people in the NEWS

Barack Obama

by Sherri Devaney, Mark Devaney,
and Michael V. Uschan

LUCENT BOOKS
A part of Gale, Cengage Learning

GALE
CENGAGE Learning

Detroit • New York • San Francisco • New Haven, Conn • Waterville, Maine • London

GALE
CENGAGE Learning™

LIBRARY OF CONGRESS CATALOGING-IN-PUBLICATION DATA

Devaney, Sherri.
    Barack Obama / by Sherri Devaney, Mark Devaney, and Michael V. Uschan.
        p. cm. — (People in the news)
    Includes bibliographical references and index.
    ISBN 978-1-4205-0206-0 (hardcover)
    1. Obama, Barack—Juvenile literature. 2. Legislators—United States—Biography—Juvenile literature. 3. African American legislators—Biography—Juvenile literature. 4. United States. Congress. Senate—Biography—Juvenile literature. 5. Racially mixed people—United States—Biography—Juvenile literature. I. Devaney, Mark. II. Uschan, Michael V., 1948- III. Title.
    E901.1.O23D488 2009
    973.932092—dc22
    [B]
                                                                        2009004314

Lucent Books
27500 Drake Rd.
Farmington Hills, MI 48331

ISBN-13: 978-1-4205-0206-0
ISBN-10: 1-4205-0206-9

Printed in the United States of America
1 2 3 4 5 6 7 13 12 11 10 09

Contents

F ame and celebrity are alluring. People are drawn to those who walk in fame's spotlight, whether they are known for great accomplishments or for notorious deeds. The lives of the famous pique public interest and attract attention, perhaps because their experiences seem in some ways so different from, yet in other ways so similar to, our own.

Newspapers, magazines, and television regularly capitalize on this fascination with celebrity by running profiles of famous people. For example, television programs such as *Entertainment Tonight* devote all of their programming to stories about entertainment and entertainers. Magazines such as *People* fill their pages with stories of the private lives of famous people. Even newspapers, newsmagazines, and television news frequently delve into the lives of well-known personalities. Despite the number of articles and programs, few provide more than a superficial glimpse at their subjects.

Lucent's People in the News series offers young readers a deeper look into the lives of today's newsmakers, the influences that have shaped them, and the impact they have had in their fields of endeavor and on other people's lives. The subjects of the series hail from many disciplines and walks of life. They include authors, musicians, athletes, political leaders, entertainers, entrepreneurs, and others who have made a mark on modern life and who, in many cases, will continue to do so for years to come.

These biographies are more than factual chronicles. Each book emphasizes the contributions, accomplishments, or deeds that have brought fame or notoriety to the individual and shows how that person has influenced modern life. Authors portray their subjects in a realistic, unsentimental light. For example, Bill Gates—the cofounder and chief executive officer of the software giant Microsoft—has been instrumental in making personal computers the most vital tool of the modern age. Few dispute his business savvy, his perseverance, or his technical expertise, yet critics say he is ruthless in his dealings with competitors and driven more by his desire to maintain Microsoft's dominance in the computer industry than by an interest in furthering technology.

In these books, young readers will encounter inspiring stories about real people who achieved success despite enormous obstacles. Oprah Winfrey—the most powerful, most watched, and wealthiest woman on television today—spent the first six years of her life in the care of her grandparents while her unwed mother sought work and a better life elsewhere. Her adolescence was colored by promiscuity, pregnancy at age fourteen, rape, and sexual abuse.

Each author documents and supports his or her work with an array of primary and secondary source quotations taken from diaries, letters, speeches, and interviews. All quotes are footnoted to show readers exactly how and where biographers derive their information and provide guidance for further research. The quotations enliven the text by giving readers eyewitness views of the life and accomplishments of each person covered in the People in the News series.

In addition, each book in the series includes photographs, annotated bibliographies, timelines, and comprehensive indexes. For both the casual reader and the student researcher, the People in the News series offers insight into the lives of today's newsmakers—people who shape the way we live, work, and play in the modern age.

The First African American President

On January 20, 2009, Barack Hussein Obama took the oath of office as the forty-fourth president of the United States of America. Obama's short but elegant inaugural address was somber because of the immense problems he would face as president, from the nation's worst economic crisis since the Great Depression in the 1920s to ongoing wars in Iraq and Afghanistan. But Obama's speech was also filled with hope that the nation could and would conquer those crises as it had so many others in its past. Obama declared:

> Forty-four Americans have now taken the presidential oath. The words have been spoken during rising tides of prosperity and the still waters of peace. Yet, every so often the oath is taken amidst gathering clouds and raging storms. At these moments, America has carried on not simply because of the skill or vision of those in high office, but because We the People have remained faithful to the ideals of our forbears, and true to our founding documents. So it has been. So it must be with this generation of Americans.[1]

Obama spoke on the west steps of the Capitol. From there, his words echoed through loudspeakers across Washington's National Mall, which stretches 1.9 miles (3km) from the Capitol to the Lincoln Memorial. They were heard by a record inaugural crowd of 1.8 million people who had traveled from every state and many countries around the world to witness history being made.

In addition to being the forty-fourth president, and a symbol of hope for a troubled country, Obama is also the first African American president of the United States. His election is historically significant because it is the fulfillment of a most sacred ideal expressed by America's founders in the Declaration of Independence, the document that declares to the entire world that "We hold these truths to be self-evident, that all men are created equal."[2] On the day a black man became president, those words seemed to be truer than ever before in the nation's history.

The Past Meets the Present

When Thomas Jefferson wrote the Declaration of Independence in 1776, a half-million black men, women, and children were slaves and did not share in that promise of equality. The United

On January 20, 2009, Barack Obama takes the oath of office from Chief Justice John Roberts to become the forty-fourth president of the United States.

States failed to extend that promise of equality to millions of African Americans by allowing slavery to continue until the end of the Civil War nine decades later in 1865. The Capitol building that loomed behind Obama as he spoke was itself a grim relic of the nation's slave past—it was built largely by slave labor, as was the White House, the presidential home in which Obama and his family now live.

Those historic buildings, however, were not the only bitter reminders of slavery that day in the nation's capital. The National Mall, on which nearly 2 million people gathered to witness Obama's inauguration, had once been the site of slave markets in which African Americans were bought and sold. Slavery is also intimately connected to the presidency itself. George Washington, the nation's first president, was a slave owner as were several other presidents, including Thomas Jefferson and Andrew Jackson. Many slaves worked as cooks and servants in the White House, and the second child born in the White House was the child of Fanny and Eddy, two slaves whom Jefferson owned.

In addition, many people in the giant inaugural crowd were descendants of slaves, including the new president's wife, Michelle, and daughters Malia and Sasha. The new First Lady's great-great-grandfather had toiled as a slave on a South Carolina rice plantation before the Civil War. But even after slavery was abolished, many whites still considered African Americans inferior and used racist laws to deny them basic rights. For another century, blacks in many states were denied one of the most basic and important rights citizens have—the right to vote. Other laws barred them from entering restaurants, stores, and even public bathrooms, because these places were reserved for whites.

Blacks were denied their civil rights and any chance for equality until the civil rights movement in the 1960s. The movement was waged by black leaders like Martin Luther King Jr. and tens of thousands of African Americans and their white supporters. The dramatic protests they staged to confront racist officials and citizens in southern states finally forced the federal government to pass legislation that outlawed racial discrimination and gave blacks the same rights as whites.

Obama is not a descendant of slaves. His ancestors lived in Africa until his father came to the United States in 1959. But in his inaugural address, Obama talked about the discrimination that his father might have faced upon arriving in America because of the racism that still existed. He said that the reason the nation ended the injustice was due to the high ideals that the United States is founded on:

This is the meaning of our liberty and our creed, why men and women and children of every race and every faith can join in celebration across this magnificent mall. And why a man whose father less than 60 years ago might not have been served at a local restaurant can now stand before you to take a most sacred oath.[3]

A Dream Fulfilled

In one of those coincidences of history, Obama's inauguration came one day after the annual national holiday to honor Martin Luther King Jr. People who came to witness the inauguration were gathered in the same place where King had given his own historic speech more than three decades earlier. On August 28, 1963, King told 250,000 black and white people who had assembled to protest racism that he had a dream. King said he longed to see the time "when all of God's children, black men and white men, Jews and Gentiles, Protestants and Catholics, will be able to join hands and sing in the words of the old Negro spiritual, 'Free at last! Free at last! Thank God Almighty, we are free at last.'"[4]

Reverend Rick Warren was one of many people at Obama's inauguration who remembered King's famous words. In a formal prayer before Obama was sworn in as president, Warren said, "We know today that Dr. King and a great cloud of witnesses are shouting [with joy] in heaven."[5] Like many people, Warren believes Obama's election is a sign that King's dream is finally coming true.

J.C. Watts is an African American who was a U.S. representative from Oklahoma from 1995 to 2003. He believes Obama's presidency is a historic step forward for the United States in

"Yes we can" became a mantra for Obama's presidential campaign. It stood for change, and for overcoming the challenges, old and new, facing the United States in the 2000s.

realizing the country's promise of equality for all people and shedding its racist past. Said Watts: "When slaves were helping to build the Capitol and the White House there might have been a flutter of hope somewhere that someday America would live out the true meaning of its creation. [Now] it has happened."[6]

Chapter 1

A Fateful Beginning

Many political leaders are born into families that possess wealth, connections to powerful people, and a cultural background that reflects mainstream America. And then there is Barack Obama, who grew up humbly, without friends or family in high places, and, most notably, came from an improbable mix of cultures. Yet despite the fact that he does not fit the mold of a typical politician, Obama is considered by many to be one of the most interesting and dynamic figures to emerge on the American political scene in the last thirty years.

Obama's ancestry as well as his unique personal history explain why he has been able to appeal to a broad spectrum of the populace and gain a growing reputation as a man who can bring people together and perhaps change the United States and even the world. Indeed, there are high expectations for Obama. Few people dispute the fact that he has the talent, knowledge, and character to accomplish great things, and a look at his past shows that he has already endured circumstances that would have prevented many other people from achieving success.

Two Vastly Different Worlds

Barack Hussein Obama Jr. is the son of two people from vastly different parts of the world. His father, Barack Obama Sr., was from Kenya, born a member of the Luo tribe on the shores of Lake Victoria in a place called Alego. His mother, S. Ann Dunham, was born in Kansas.

A bright child, Barack Obama Sr. tended goats on his father's farm until he earned a sponsorship to attend a university in the United States. In 1959, at the age of twenty-three, he became the University of Hawaii's first African student. It was there that he met eighteen-year-old Dunham, who was also a student at the university.

Dunham was a smart but shy, only child. She was actually named Stanley Ann, after her father, Stanley Dunham, a man whose interests and energy led their small family to move around the country frequently as he sought better jobs and a better way of life. Born and raised in Kansas, Stanley Dunham (or "Gramps," as young Barack called him) was a soldier in World War II who never experienced combat. Ann was born at the army base where

Born into Kenya's Luo tribe (members are pictured here), Barack Obama Sr. would later attend the University of Hawaii as the school's first African student.

Cultures Collide

Although the Dunhams never prospered, they did provide Ann with a stable home. They were open-minded parents, but their tolerance was tested when eighteen-year-old Ann informed them that she wanted to marry a twenty-three-year-old black man from another continent. Yet neither Stanley nor Madelyn could deny that Ann was truly in love, and Barack Obama Sr.'s intellect and charm quickly won them over.

Barack Obama Sr.'s father, Hussein, was less agreeable to the match. Shortly before the wedding, he wrote a letter to Stanley Dunham from Africa saying that he did not approve of the marriage. One reason for this, according to Ann, was that Hussein did not want the Obama blood to be "sullied by a white woman."[9] Barack Obama Sr. wrote back to Hussein informing him that he was going forward with the wedding, and he married Ann in a small civil ceremony in 1960. Barack Hussein Obama Jr. was born shortly thereafter on August 4, 1961.

Barack Obama Sr. continued with his education, and upon graduation from the University of Hawaii with a degree in economics that he had earned in only three years, he received two scholarships for graduate school. One was from the New School in New York City and would have provided him with full tuition, along with room and board for Ann and the baby. The second scholarship, from Harvard University in Massachusetts, provided only full tuition for Obama Sr. According to Ann, while deciding which offer to accept, Obama Sr. received harsh news from his father. Hussein was adamant in his rejection of Ann. He threatened to have his son's student visa revoked, which would have forced Obama Sr. to return to Africa before completing his graduate studies. The pressure from Hussein, coupled with his own overwhelming desire to attend a university as prestigious as Harvard, led Obama Sr. to choose the Ivy League school. He left for Massachusetts in 1963 to pursue his studies. Ann remained in Hawaii with their two-year-old son. The couple eventually divorced.

Thus, early in his life, before he was even aware of it, Barack Obama Jr. was different from other children in many ways. Half-black, half-white, and essentially fatherless, he already could not be neatly categorized into one ethnicity or demographic.

Lessons from Indonesia

Barack Obama Jr.'s life soon took another turn. About two years after the senior Obama left, Ann met Lolo Soetoro, a University of Hawaii student from Indonesia, a Southeast Asian country comprising several islands in the Indian and Pacific oceans. After dating Soetoro for two years, Ann accepted his proposal of marriage. Soon after the couple married, Soetoro returned to his homeland, but unlike Barack Obama Sr., he took his new bride and her now six-year-old son with him. Obama, who was called "Barry" as a child, lived in Indonesia for four years. There, his mother gave birth to his half sister, Maya.

While living in Indonesia, Obama came to understand how the United States, unlike many other countries, offers numerous opportunities as an economically free society. Even as a young child, he observed that people in Indonesia are born into families whose lot in life is dictated by their economic class, and it is extremely difficult to ascend into a higher economic class. In the United States, by contrast, all people have the freedoms of life, liberty, and the pursuit of happiness regardless of their race, gender, or class.

Obama was also exposed to poverty in Indonesia, where many families struggled daily to obtain enough food. People lived modestly in ramshackle homes where it was common to see chickens and livestock roaming in yards. Later in life, Obama drew parallels between what he witnessed in Indonesia and what he witnessed in American inner cities.

During his time in Indonesia, Obama also began to learn about his African American heritage. His mother regularly provided him with reading materials about the treatment of African Americans in the United States. She taught him about the nation's history of slavery and the more recent fight for civil rights. She made sure that her son knew of the great contributions made by black leaders in politics, history, culture, music, and sports. Obama describes her message in his memoir: "To be black was to be the beneficiary of a great inheritance, a special destiny, glorious burdens that only we were strong enough to bear."[10]

But the pride his mother passed on to young Obama was tempered by his growing awareness of issues surrounding race. Most disturbing was the self-hatred among some African Americans due to their skin color. Obama came upon the subject while reading a *Life* magazine story about a black man who had tried to peel off his skin to look white. It had never occurred to Obama that people would feel so ashamed of their skin color that they would take such drastic and dangerous steps to undo nature, but the article changed his understanding of race. He explains in his memoir, "I began to notice . . . that there was nobody like me in the Sears, Roebuck Christmas catalog that Toot and Gramps sent us, and that Santa was a white man. . . . I still trusted my mother's love—but I now faced the prospect that her account of the world, and my father's place in it, was somehow incomplete."[11]

Living in Indonesia in the 1960s, young Obama was moved by the plight of the country's poor, who had little chance of improving their lot.

Punahou Academy

After four years of living in Indonesia, Obama was sent back to Hawaii to live with Toot and Gramps and enter the fifth grade at Punahou Academy, an elite Hawaiian prep school. His grandparents were only too happy to accommodate him. They were proud that their grandchild was a student at such a well-respected educational institution.

Having been away from the United States for so long, Obama felt out of place at Punahou. The majority of other students had attended school together since kindergarten. Most of them came from well-to-do families and had better-quality and more-stylish clothes than Obama. He was one of only two black children in his class, and other students mocked his foreign name. Instead of feeling proud of his Kenyan heritage, Obama often felt conflicted, even embarrassed by his differences from the other children.

Obama attended prep school in Honolulu, Hawaii, at the prestigious Punahou Academy.

As Obama sought to fit in among his classmates, he received some startling news. Barack Obama Sr. had been in a serious car accident in Kenya, and he was coming for a month-long visit to recuperate after a lengthy stay in the hospital.

Tense Visit

The young Obama was nervous about meeting his father. His mother and grandparents had told him that his father was a brilliant diplomat doing important work to help his country, but young Obama still felt he knew little about him. Sometimes he felt proud that his father was a leader in Kenya trying to improve life for his countrymen. But at other times, Obama could not understand why his father was not with him.

The visit was awkward and confusing. Young Obama was impressed with his father, but the man was a stranger to him. The boy knew that his father was intelligent and worldly, but he was also strict, criticizing his son for watching too much television and for not studying more. Education had been the key to Barack Obama Sr.'s escaping an impoverished life. Young Obama was not as desperate to learn as his father had been, and this led to tension during their brief time together.

The elder Obama's visit created tension for his son in another way as well. Young Obama had grown up different, a black child being raised by white grandparents in a state populated by Hawaiians. He feared that being exposed as the son of an African who spoke with a strange accent would only emphasize the contrast between himself and other children in Hawaii.

One event in particular characterized the conflicted emotions that Obama had for his father. When Obama's teacher learned that his father was in Hawaii, she invited him to speak to her class. Obama dreaded the day because he expected his classmates to tease him afterward. His fear turned to pride, however, as the man from Africa held the students transfixed. Obama describes what happened:

> He spoke of the wild animals that still roamed the plains, the tribes that still required a young boy to kill a lion to prove his manhood. . . . He told us of Kenya's struggle to be free, how

the British had wanted to stay and unjustly rule the people, just as they had in America; how they had been enslaved only because of the color of their skin, just as they had in America; but that Kenyans . . . longed to be free and develop themselves through hard work and sacrifice.[12]

Obama's father stayed for only one month. Soon after he returned to Africa, Obama's mother, now separated from Soetoro, came back to Hawaii to pursue a master's degree in anthropology. Obama lived in an apartment a block from the Punahou Academy with his mother and his sister, Maya, for the next three years.

Triumph and Tragedy

After Barack Obama Sr. divorced Ann Dunham and returned to Africa, he married a white woman whose father worked in the Kenyan embassy. For some time he did well working for an American oil company. Kenya gained its independence from England in 1963, and Obama Sr. was connected with all the top government people, which led him to take a high-ranking job with the Ministry of Tourism.

Obama Sr. was still with the Ministry of Tourism in 1966, when a division grew between two Kenyan tribes: the Kikuyu, led by President Jomo Kenyatta, and the Luo, Obama Sr.'s tribe. The Luo tribe complained that Kikuyu tribe members were getting the best jobs in the country, and Obama Sr. protested publicly about the issue. His outspokenness caused him to be banished from the government. His passport was revoked, so he could not leave Kenya to find other opportunities abroad. During this time, his wife left him. He began to drink and fell into near poverty for many years.

Eventually the political situation in Kenya changed, and Obama Sr. was able to return to government work in the Ministry of Finance. Tragically, just as his life was beginning to improve, he was killed in a car accident in 1982, when Obama Jr. was twenty-one.

Teenage Struggles with Identity

When his mother made plans to return to Indonesia once again—this time to complete her fieldwork for her graduate degree—Obama elected to stay at Punahou and to once again live with his grandparents. During these years Obama's internal conflicts about his identity grew. His mixed heritage created conflict when he befriended blacks who voiced their resentment of whites. He was privy to such comments because those who made them did not know that his mother was white. In an interview with talk-show host Oprah Winfrey, Obama described his inner turmoil:

> There was a level of . . . a divided identity. One that was inside the home and one was to the outside world. . . . And I think it was reconciling those two things, the understanding that I can be African American and proud of that heritage and proud of that culture and part of that community and yet not be limited by it. And that . . . that's not exclusive of my love for my mother or my love for my grandparents, that I can be part of the same thing.[13]

Obama's personal conflicts along with typical teen rebelliousness led him to wayward behavior. He drank, smoked marijuana, and even used cocaine. Although he never became addicted to hard drugs, he did develop a cigarette smoking habit that would plague him for years.

Obama frequently sought refuge on the basketball court. He found acceptance and belonging there, first playing pickup basketball in park playgrounds near his home and then as a member of his high school basketball team. He recalls, "I was living out a caricature of black male adolescence, itself a caricature of swaggering American manhood. . . . At least on the basketball court I could find a community of sorts, with an inner life all its own. It was there that I would make my closest white friends, on turf where blackness couldn't be a disadvantage."[14] As Obama spent more time on social activities than academics, his grades suffered a bit, and so did his ambition. He drifted without clear direction as his high school years concluded.

Occidental College

Despite his lack of focus on his future, Obama wound up at Occidental College in Los Angeles in 1979. The criteria he used to pick the school could be construed as a whim. He chose Occidental because he had heard of the school from a girl vacationing in Hawaii from Brentwood, a Los Angeles suburb.

At Occidental, he once again grappled with issues of race. Unlike the black students from economically depressed cities, Obama could not easily identify with the plight of impoverished and disadvantaged blacks in the United States. In fact, he reflects in his memoir that he was more like "the black students who had grown up in the suburbs, kids whose parents had already paid the price of escape"[15] from inner cities. His multiracial makeup compounded his sense of estrangement from blacks, yet he was not comfortable downplaying or even disavowing his African American heritage as some multiracial students did.

In a state of limbo between black and white, Obama says his friends were

> the more politically active black students. The foreign students. The Chicanos. The Marxist professors and structural feminists and punk-rock performance poets. We smoked cigarettes and wore leather jackets. . . . When we ground out our cigarettes in the hallway carpet or set our stereos so loud that the walls began to shake, we were resisting bourgeois society's stifling constraints. We weren't indifferent or careless or insecure. We were alienated.[16]

Yet once again, Obama reached a crossroads. On one hand, he tried to assimilate what he presumed to be black thinking—rebel against white authority, even if it means doing poorly in college, because for blacks school does not matter. However, he also encountered blacks who appreciated the sacrifices that their families had made to send them to school, and they criticized him for not applying himself academically. Writer and reporter Noam Scheiber states, "Obama's eventual response to his multicultural background was neither to shun his black identity, nor to shore it up by segregating himself from whites. It was to be racially

Students sit on the library steps at Columbia University, where Obama became a student in 1981.

proud, while striving to succeed in mainstream (and predominantly white) institutions."[17]

Eventually, Obama came to the realization that he was not living up to his full potential. After two years at Occidental, he transferred to Columbia University in New York City in 1981. His childhood and adolescence over, Obama set out to find his calling.

Chapter 2

The Streets of Chicago

As a young adult, Barack Obama made a series of career moves that were impressive yet unexpected. He arrived at Columbia University eager to live in what he called "a true city, with black neighborhoods in close proximity."[18] He got his wish because the school is located only a few blocks from Harlem, a section of New York City that is home to thousands of African Americans and is rife with all the societal ills common to urban areas: poverty, drugs, violence, and homelessness.

By the time Obama completed his degree in political science with a specialization in international relations in 1983, he had decided to become a community organizer. He wanted to bring people together on a local level to promote social progress and protest unfair treatment, which could include anything from poor educational facilities, inferior housing conditions, and pollution to lost jobs and low wages for working-class citizens. According to Obama, "communities had never been a given in this country. . . . Communities had to be created, fought for, tended like gardens."[19]

Time for Change

Despite the fact that American citizens in inner cities had many problems, it was not so simple for Obama to find work as a community organizer. He submitted letters to many civil rights organizations and to black elected officials all over the country who had progressive agendas, yet no one replied.

To earn an income in the meantime, he took a research assistant job at a consulting house for a multinational corporation. He was eventually promoted to the position of financial writer. Obama now had money, his own office, and his own secretary. He describes this time in his life in his memoir:

> Sometimes coming out of an interview with Japanese financiers or German bond traders, I would catch my reflection in the elevator doors—see myself in a suit and tie, a briefcase in my hand—and for a split second I would imagine myself as a captain of industry, barking out orders, closing the deal, before I remembered who it was that I had told myself I wanted to be and felt pangs of guilt for my own lack of resolve.[20]

This guilt eventually resulted in Obama resigning his position and focusing again on finding work as a community organizer.

Obama was pleased with the proximity of Columbia University to Harlem, a largely black New York City neighborhood (pictured in 1986).

Although he got a job organizing a conference on drugs, unemployment, and housing, this role was too removed from the streets. So he took another position, this time in Harlem, trying to convince the students at City College of the importance of recycling. Then he took another low-paying assignment passing out flyers for an assemblyman's race in Brooklyn. "In six months I was broke, unemployed, eating soup from a can,"[21] he recalls. But finally an opportunity came to him that literally redirected his life.

Finding a Focus in Chicago

Obama was recruited by a labor organizer affiliated with the Calumet Community Religious Conference (CCRC), an organization formed to address the impact of factory closings and layoffs then taking place in South Chicago. Once critical to the

Obama worked with the CCRC in Chicago (pictured) to confront the issues of factory closings and layoffs in the city.

When the CCRC tried to increase job opportunities for blacks in Chicago, black church leaders—worried about appearing disrespectful to Chicago's popular black mayor, Harold Washington (center)—did not want to help.

nation's economy, Chicago's manufacturing companies, like so many others around the nation, had relocated operations—mostly overseas to take advantage of cheaper labor—or had simply gone out of business. The CCRC sought to mobilize residents through a network of twenty-eight suburban and urban churches, known as the Developing Communities Project (DCP). The objective was to bring jobs and manufacturing back to Chicago, and Obama was hired at a small annual salary in 1985 to help unite people in this common cause.

Obama found that his job was not easy. For one, he discovered that it was difficult to convince local black religious leaders to speak out for more and better jobs for African Americans, mainly because the mayor of Chicago at the time was Harold Washington, the first

African American ever elected to that position. Washington was a hero to Chicago's African Americans, and some of the church leaders did not want to be perceived as disrespectful to him.

Despite the reluctance of some of the church leaders to cooperate, Obama pressed on with a variety of issues that strayed somewhat from the mission of the DCP. For example, he held a meeting to address gang violence, but the organized event flopped. Hardly anyone showed up. Obama learned that gang violence was too big of an issue to rally people around. While people certainly wanted something to be done to improve safety in their neighborhoods, they most wanted help finding jobs. Obama learned a valuable lesson: If he was going to succeed at community organizing, he had to focus on concrete matters, such as jobs and decent housing for the working poor. Sometime thereafter he found a place to concentrate his efforts: Altgeld Gardens.

Altgeld Gardens and MET

Obama realized his first real success as a community organizer by helping to call the attention of the Mayor's Office of Employment and Training (MET) to Altgeld Gardens, a public housing project on the southern edge of the city of Chicago. Unlike high-rise projects common to most major cities, Altgeld was only two stories tall, and although the residents did not own their apartments, they took pride in their homes, despite the deplorable conditions in and around them. Obama describes Altgeld:

> The Altgeld Gardens Public Housing Project sat at Chicago's southernmost edge: two thousand apartments arranged in a series of two-story brick buildings with army-green doors and grimy mock shutters. . . . To the east . . . was the Lake Calumet landfill, the largest in the Midwest. And to the north, directly across the street, was the Metropolitan Sanitary District's sewage treatment plant. . . . The stench, the toxins, the empty uninhabited landscape. For close to a century, the few square miles surrounding Altgeld had taken in the offal of scores of factories, the price people had paid for their high-wage jobs. Now that the

jobs were gone, and those people that could had already left, it seemed only natural to use the land as a dump. A dump—and a place to house poor blacks.[22]

Obama interviewed and befriended residents of Altgeld. He learned that employment was a key issue for them, and he set out to connect the group with MET, which referred unemployed people to training programs throughout the city. He discovered that MET did not have an office anywhere near Altgeld, so he wrote to the woman in charge of the agency. She agreed to meet with a group of Altgeld Gardens residents. Obama's goal was to get a job intake and training center on the far south side of the city. He coached the residents on what to say at the meeting and made all the arrangements for it. More than one hundred people attended the event, and the director of MET could not deny that an office needed to be established in the community.

Asbestos at Altgeld

Emboldened by his triumph with MET, Obama's next challenge involved helping Altgeld residents persuade the city of Chicago to fix a problem with asbestos. Asbestos was once considered a useful product because it is fireproof. For decades asbestos was used to insulate pipes and walls in buildings and homes until it was discovered to cause cancer. A woman who lived in the Altgeld housing project showed Obama a small advertisement she had found seeking contractors to remove asbestos from an Altgeld management office site. The woman wondered if the apartments had asbestos as well.

Obama led a small contingent of residents to the building manager's office and was told that the apartments had been tested and that there was no asbestos in them. When pressed for evidence, the building manager could not deliver proof of this testing. In response, Obama and some Altgeld residents organized a bus trip to the Community Housing Authority's offices.

Obama notified the press to attend the meeting because he knew that the news media would be interested in a story about

Obama worked successfully with residents of Chicago's Altgeld Gardens housing project (pictured in 2005) to eliminate cancer-causing asbestos materials.

the possibility of a known cancer-causing material such as asbestos having a negative impact on the health of city residents. He was also confident that Community Housing Authority executives would not want to be portrayed publicly as negligent. Sure enough, with cameras rolling, they admitted that asbestos was present in the apartments of Altgeld Gardens. City officials immediately proposed a plan to remove the asbestos.

Obama felt triumphant as a result of this win and reflected on it in his memoir:

> I changed as a result of that bus trip. . . . It was the sort of change that's important not because it alters your concrete circumstances in some way . . . but because it hints at what might be possible and therefore spurs you on, beyond the immediate exhilaration, beyond any subsequent disappointments, to retrieve that thing that you once, ever so briefly, held in your hand. That bus ride kept me going, I think. Maybe it still does.[23]

From Kenya to Boston

Although Obama began to experience more victories than defeats in Chicago, he believed that he needed additional education to become more effective as a leader. So after several years as a community organizer, he decided to apply to law school. He explains what he imagined law school would teach him:

> I had things to learn in law school, things that would help me bring about real change. I would learn about interest rates, corporate mergers, the legislative process; about the way businesses and banks were put together; how real estate ventures succeeded or failed. I would learn power's currency in all its intricacy and detail, knowledge that would have compromised me before coming to Chicago but that I could now bring back to where it was needed . . . back to Altgeld; bring it back like Promethean fire.[24]

As he had hoped, Obama was accepted into Harvard Law School. Before leaving for Boston to attend Harvard, Obama decided to travel to Kenya to learn more about his family. He spent

Before entering law school, Obama visited relatives in Kenya, including his grandmother, Onyango Obama (pictured in 2004).

time with aunts, uncles, and cousins whom he met for the first time, and he had the opportunity to meet his Kenyan grandmother, Onyango Obama. All of these relatives told him stories of his father and grandfather. According to author and acquaintance Scott Turow, it was in Kenya that Obama "managed to fully embrace a heritage and a family he'd never fully known and come to terms with his father, whom he'd long regarded as an august foreign prince, but now realized was a human being burdened by his own illusions and vulnerabilities."[25]

Upon his return from Kenya in the fall of 1988, Obama entered Harvard Law School. He excelled there and became the first African American president of the prestigious *Harvard Law Review* in 1990. During this time, his potential as a political leader was obvious, especially to his professors, including Laurence Tribe, who taught constitutional law. In an article in *Time* magazine, Tribe states, "I've known Senators, Presidents. I've never known anyone with what seems to me more raw political talent. He [Obama] just seems to have the surest way of calmly reaching across what are impenetrable barriers to many people."[26]

While on leave from Harvard to work as a summer associate at a downtown Chicago firm, Obama met Michelle Robinson. Robinson, also a graduate of Harvard Law School, had earned her undergraduate degree at Princeton University, where her brother was a basketball star. She came from a working-class African American family in Chicago. *New Yorker* staff writer William Finnegan states, "[Obama] turned out to have little interest in corporate law but plenty of interest in Michelle."[27] After their engagement, Obama visited Kenya again, this time with Robinson.

Obama graduated magna cum laude (with highest honors) from Harvard Law School in 1991 and was sought after by several prominent law firms. Moreover, Abner Mikva, a former five-term congressman for Illinois who was chief judge of the U.S. Court of Appeals for the D.C. circuit, tried to recruit Obama as a clerk, a position "considered a stepping stone to clerking on the Supreme Court,"[28] according to Finnegan. But Obama turned down the judge. Unlike many people in his situation who would have chosen the pursuit of money and power, Obama wanted to return to the roots he had put down in Chicago's South Side.

The *Harvard Law Review*

Published since 1887, the *Harvard Law Review* is one of the most prestigious journals of legal scholarship in the United States. It was created by Louis Brandeis, a Harvard Law School alumnus and Boston attorney who went on to become a justice on the U.S. Supreme Court. The purpose of the *Harvard Law Review* is to be an effective research tool for practicing lawyers and students of the law. Additionally, it provides opportunities for law students to write their own articles, which typically take the form of comments about cases or recent court decisions. Run by students, the monthly *Harvard Law Review* averages two thousand pages per volume and reaches eight thousand subscribers, an audience comprising attorneys, judges, and professors.

Each year about ten student candidates run for the position of president of the *Harvard Law Review*. Staff of the review then elect the candidate best qualified to lead the publication. It is an extremely competitive process. Before Barack Obama in 1991, no African American had ever attained the position, which has served as the launching pad for the careers of some of the most prominent legal minds in America.

Obama is pictured following his election as president of the Harvard Law Review.

Back to Chicago

After graduating from Harvard Law School, Obama married Robinson in 1992. The ceremony was bittersweet for the couple: Robinson's father died before he could give his daughter away, and Gramps, Obama's maternal grandfather, had recently lost his life to prostate cancer. The newlyweds moved into the Hyde Park neighborhood on Chicago's South Side. They eventually had two daughters: Malia, born in 1999, and Sasha, born in 2001.

As a Chicago resident once again, Obama became director of the Illinois Project Vote, helping to register one hundred thousand mostly minority, low-income Democratic voters from April to November 1992. His efforts helped Bill Clinton carry Illinois in the 1992 presidential election, and Carol Moseley Braun become the first African American woman to be elected to the U.S. Senate.

In 1993 a small, public-interest law firm hired Obama. There, he worked as a civil rights attorney, specializing in employment discrimination, fair housing, and voting-rights litigation. That same year he was named in *Crain's* magazine's list of "40 under 40" outstanding young leaders in the city of Chicago. He also became a lecturer at the University of Chicago Law School.

In 1996 Obama launched his political career when he ran for and won election to the Illinois state senate. As a state senator, Obama focused his efforts on helping working families. One way he did this was to collaborate with Democrats and Republicans

In a 2004 photo, Obama and his wife, Michelle, relax with their daughters, Sasha and Malia.

All's Fair

In 1996 Illinois state senator Alice Palmer offered Barack Obama a chance to run for state senator in the thirteenth district, where he and Michelle lived. Palmer had decided that she wanted to run for Congress, but when she lost the primary election, she changed her mind and decided to seek reelection as a state senator. Obama, whose campaign was already in full swing, declined to step aside, claiming that Palmer promised him she would not seek reelection. When Obama's supporters challenged Palmer's petitions, she withdrew and ended her political career.

Some political activists in Illinois felt that Obama was overly ambitious and should have stepped aside and allowed the more experienced senator to continue the effective work she was doing. Obama was not eager to discuss Palmer, telling a *Chicago Sun-Times* reporter in 2004, "My preference would be not to revisit it too deeply." He also said, "I can tell you that it was an unfortunate situation, but one in which I operated completely aboveboard."

Quoted in Scott Forneck, "Obama: 'I've Got a Competitive Nature,'" *Chicago Sun-Times*, October 3, 2004.

alike to create programs, such as the state earned-income tax credit. The refundable tax credit reduces or eliminates the amount of taxes that low-income people pay; in three years this program provided more than $100 million in tax cuts to families in Illinois. Obama also pushed through an expansion of early childhood education and helped broaden a state health insurance program for children who were otherwise uninsured.

Crushed by Rush

After nearly four years of serving as a state senator, Obama attempted to become a member of the U.S. House of Representatives by running against incumbent Bobby Rush in 2000. Rush

In 2000 incumbent Bobby Rush (seen in 2006) soundly defeated Obama in the Illinois congressional election.

was active during the civil rights movement of the 1960s and was popular among local residents. In 1968 he helped found the Illinois Black Panther Party, a radical group whose occasional militaristic activities attracted the attention of the government and local law enforcement. Rush, however, had also helped his fellow inner-city residents through peaceful and law-abiding means. His record showed improvements in health care and the environment as well as the passage of strong gun-control measures and the implementation of programs that spurred economic development.

Indeed, Rush had been successful in accomplishing many of the social reforms that Obama had been seeking to enact. Yet more important than Rush's seniority and track record was the perceptual advantage he held over Obama. According to Noam Scheiber, Rush's frequent intimations that Obama was not "black enough . . . that he [had not] been around the first congressional district long enough to really see what's going on,"[29] and that Obama was an elitist, were difficult to combat. There was little Obama could do to reverse these perceptions, and Rush defeated him, receiving 61 percent of the vote to Obama's 30 percent.

Ups and Downs in the State Senate

After losing to Rush, Obama refocused his attention and talents in the Illinois state senate. Yet even there he suffered a significant political setback. The Republicans were prepared to fight strongly against a gun-control bill, and the Democrats needed Obama's skills and influence to help their side. At the time, Obama was in Hawaii visiting relatives, when his younger daughter became sick. Torn between his obligations to his family and to the state senate, Obama chose to stay in Hawaii with his daughter, and the bill was defeated. Obama's explanation for his absence, according to Turow, "did not play either with the press . . . or his fellow politicians, who'd left plenty of sickbeds and vacations in their time for the sake of public duty."[30]

Nevertheless, Obama carried on in the state senate. He worked to make sure that certain ethnic or minority groups were not unfairly targeted for criminal prosecution and to prevent wrongful convictions in death-penalty cases. After a number of inmates on death row were found innocent, Obama, with the help of law enforcement officials, drafted legislation that required the videotaping of interrogations and confessions in all murder cases. Obama explains some of the benefits of such legislation in a *Daily Herald* newspaper article: "Rather than impeding law enforcement, it has made it more simple to prosecute criminals and ensure accuracy in their prosecution."[31] Even as opponents cited the plan as too costly for most police departments, Obama's proposal was approved.

Obama remained fearless in embracing unpopular causes. David Mendell reports in the *Chicago Tribune* that Obama was "one of just nine senators to vote against a bill that toughened penalties for violent crimes committed during gang activity." Obama opposed the bill because the law did not clearly define a gang member, and he questioned why lawmakers were "targeting Hispanics and blacks for stiffer sentences."[32]

Obama also wrote and worked hard to gather support from both political parties for a bill that required law enforcement personnel to keep track of the race of drivers they pulled over for traffic stops. According to Finnegan, this was not necessarily a wise political move because stopping racial profiling was "not a popular issue outside minority communities."[33]

Yet it was precisely the type of issue that Obama seemed uniquely suited to address, and his career progressed unabated. With his abilities as a lawmaker growing, and wiser from his ill-advised run for the House of Representatives, Obama next set his sights on the U.S. Senate.

Chapter 3

Senator Obama

As Obama prepared to take his career to the national level, he had no way of knowing that he was about to benefit from circumstances beyond his control. Even though he had earned an education from two excellent universities and had worked hard at the grassroots level to gain practical experience, he was aided as well by his political opponents' missteps, which helped clear the way for him to become a U.S. senator.

Setting the Stage

Ironically, in order for Obama to become only the third African American to be elected a U.S. senator, Carol Moseley Braun, the second African American and the only African American woman ever elected senator, had to make some mistakes. Born and educated in urban Chicago, Moseley Braun had held local political positions for six years, but her one term in the Senate was marked with controversy. Although never convicted, Moseley Braun was plagued by allegations of misappropriating campaign expenditures. She and Kgosie Matthews, her fiancé and campaign manager, were accused of using campaign funds to take long and costly trips to places including South Africa, Nigeria, and Hawaii. These travels appeared to be more personal than political. The accusations, along with widespread reports about sloppy bookkeeping, damaged Moseley Braun's reputation and opened the door for a Republican challenger named Peter Fitzgerald in the 1998 Senate election.

On election night in 1998, incumbent senator Carol Moseley Braun crosses her fingers for luck, but loses to challenger Peter Fitzgerald.

In a state such as Illinois, which largely votes Democratic, it was unlikely that a Republican like Fitzgerald could defeat Moseley Braun. But because of the stories about Moseley Braun's accounting troubles, Fitzgerald, who promoted himself as an outsider to Illinois politics, was able to defeat Moseley Braun 51 percent to 47 percent, thus becoming the first Republican senator from Chicago in twenty years.

Fitzgerald, an independent thinker, drew criticism from his own party for not supporting more staunchly conservative positions on issues like the environment. For example, he was against exploratory oil drilling in Alaska. He also argued for the appointment of an independent U.S. attorney to investigate corruption in Illinois state government, which resulted in the eventual indictment of Republican governor George Ryan. These beliefs and actions made Fitzgerald an outsider in his own party. Sensing this, he declined to run for a second term as senator. Therefore, Moseley Braun's mistakes and Fitzgerald's maverick personality set the stage for a memorable campaign for the open Senate seat in 2004.

The Senate Democratic Primary

Still a state senator, Barack Obama decided to run for the national position, but he was not favored to win the Democratic primary. Initially, Marson Blair Hull Jr., a businessman turned politician, was the leading Democratic candidate. Hull made millions of dollars selling his investment company, the Hull Group, to Goldman Sachs, a global investment bank. His wealth enabled him to contribute

Leaving a Chicago church after an appearance during his 2004 U.S. Senate campaign, Obama stops to give his daughter a kiss.

more than $28 million of his own money to his campaign, which gave him a substantial lead in the polls, mostly because of an expensive advertising blitz.

Illinois comptroller Dan Hynes was another Democratic candidate. Hynes came from a powerful political family and had the support of labor unions, which traditionally were part of the so-called machine that exerted great clout during Illinois elections. Conventional wisdom held that to win an election, a candidate had to gain the support of labor union leaders, who then directed union members how to vote. Therefore, by getting the support of one union leader, a politician would theoretically be earning thousands of votes. However, according to David Axelrod, Obama's campaign manager, "a few creaky parts [of the machine] still work. . . . They can still elect a few water commissioners or sub-circuit-level judges. But no precinct captain [from a labor union] can tell people how to vote for President or the Senate."[34]

As he campaigned against Hynes and Hull, Obama began to use his biracial heritage to his advantage. He could connect with urban blacks and at the same time build a rapport with suburban and rural white voters, which was unprecedented for a minority candidate. Furthermore, Obama earned support from what New Yorker staff writer William Finnegan called "lakefront liberals—residents of the city's swankier boroughs, most of them white professionals."[35] One reason why this influential, well-educated, and politically savvy group favored Obama was his outspoken opposition to the war in Iraq.

Despite growing interest in and support for Obama, he was trailing Hull late in the campaign until a story surfaced alleging that Hull had physically abused his former wife. These charges hurt Hull politically, and his lead over Obama shrank. At the same time, Obama secured endorsements from prominent leaders, such as former Democratic national chairman David Wilhelm as well as from the Chicago Tribune and the Chicago Sun-Times. Campaign manager Axelrod crafted an advertising strategy that drew parallels between Obama and beloved Illinois Democrats, including the late senator Paul Simon and the late Harold Washington, Chicago's first black mayor. Because of the scandal surrounding Hull and the momentum created by his own campaign, Obama won the primary held in March 2004, earning 53 percent of the vote, more than all of the other Democratic candidates combined.

A Formidable Republican Opponent

Winning the Democratic primary was only half the battle, however; next would come the general election and a formidable Republican opponent named Jack Ryan. Like Hull, Ryan had used a great deal of his own money to finance his primary campaign. And like Obama, Ryan was young, handsome, and Harvard educated. He had earned a master's degree in business administration from Harvard Business School and a law degree from Harvard Law School. Moreover, like Obama, Ryan did more than talk about

Pictured after winning the Republican nomination for the Illinois senate in 2004, Jack Ryan is poised to face Democrat Barack Obama in the general election.

helping the underprivileged in urban Chicago. Ryan left his lucrative finance job with Goldman Sachs to teach at an inner-city Chicago parochial high school.

Yet despite their similarities, Ryan and Obama were vastly different in terms of political philosophy. Ryan, more so than even the most conservative Republicans, believed in cutting taxes for all citizens, especially high-income earners. He was against gun control and abortion and in favor of school vouchers, which would enable parents to send their children to school districts other than their own to take advantage of better school systems.

Ryan portrayed himself as being consistent in his beliefs in part because he thought he could unearth inconsistencies in Obama's voting record. He also tried to catch Obama making contradictory promises on the campaign trail. Ryan ordered Justin Warfel, a young campaign staffer, to follow Obama everywhere he went and videotape his statements. The objective was to capture Obama on videotape saying one thing to one audience, then promising the complete opposite to another audience. The tactic backfired, however, after Warfel was observed shouting questions in Obama's face and recording Obama's personal conversations with his wife and daughters.

Ryan's Scandal

Ryan's campaign fell apart when lurid details about his relationship with his former wife, actress Jeri Ryan, became public. A popular celebrity in her own right because of starring roles on television shows such as *Star Trek: Voyager* and *Boston Public*, Jeri married Ryan in 1991. The couple had a son, but their demanding careers began to take a toll on their marriage. With Jack in Chicago and Jeri living in Los Angeles, frequent separations caused them to drift apart. They divorced in 1999, five years before the U.S. Senate campaign.

The couple agreed to release divorce papers to the public but requested that child custody files be kept private to protect their son. However, the *Chicago Tribune*, in conjunction with WLS-TV and the local ABC affiliate, conducted an investigation into rumors surrounding the Ryan divorce and pressed the court for more information. In a controversial decision on June 22, 2004, a California judge agreed to release the custody files to the press against the wishes of Jack and Jeri Ryan. The documents contained sexually explicit details about the couple, and the media seized upon the scandalous content, which ruined Ryan's campaign and forced him to withdraw his candidacy for senator. This left the Illinois Republican Party scrambling for a replacement to take on Obama, who was already leading in the polls against Ryan but was now suddenly running unchallenged.

In Comes Keyes

With no Republican challenger to Obama, the Illinois State Republican Committee went beyond state borders to recruit a nationally known African American conservative named Alan Keyes. By this time, Obama's popularity was surging, so Keyes faced an uphill battle trying to convince Illinois residents to vote for him, especially given the fact that he did not even live in their state. Ironically, in 2000 Keyes had publicly criticized former First Lady Hillary Rodham Clinton for running for senator of New York since she was not a native of the state and had only recently moved there. Nonetheless, Keyes accepted the invitation to run against Obama in Illinois despite the fact that he lived in Maryland.

As an African American conservative, Keyes has always drawn attention to himself, which has both helped and hurt his career. Race has invariably been a major issue for Keyes because he rejects many beliefs on race, education, equal rights, and religion that are widely held by other African Americans. For example, Keyes is against affirmative action, a policy that requires state-funded institutions, such as universities and government agencies, to accept or hire a proportionate number of minorities. Furthermore, he has often complained that the media does not give him enough coverage because of his race and views. In an interview on the political television program *Crossfire*, Keyes stated, "I don't correspond to the stereotype, so they're pushing me out. A conservative black American is somebody who simply doesn't correspond to what the media believes black people ought to be."[36]

Alan Keyes

Alan Keyes' career included a stint in the U.S. State Department, diplomatic positions in India and Zimbabwe, and several important ambassadorial jobs. But Keyes truly came to be known during his failed run for the Republican presidential nomination against George W. Bush and Senator John McCain in 2000. Although he had little chance of defeating either opponent, Keyes managed to remain in the campaign long enough to be invited to participate in several nationally televised debates. The country had not seen an African American politician voice such staunchly conservative opinions before, and many viewers were impressed with him. After bowing out of the election, he parlayed his sudden fame into a talk-radio career with his own show, *Alan Keyes Is Making Sense*. The show did not last long, but it enabled Keyes to air his controversial opinions and kept him in the national spotlight until the Republican Party of Illinois asked him to run against Obama.

Yet it was precisely because of his conservatism that the Illinois State Republican Committee believed Keyes could challenge Obama, whose more liberal opinions made for a sharp contrast between the two candidates. In fact, one of Keyes' strategies, much like Ryan's, was to portray Obama as radically liberal on the major issues. Bill Pascoe, Keyes' spokesman, compared Obama's political leanings to other well-known Democrats:

> Were [Obama] to be elected to the United States Senate, he would be to the left of Hillary Clinton on abortion, left of Ted Kennedy on health care, to the left of John Kerry on taxes, to the left of Howard Dean on the war. It will be one of the goals of the Keyes campaign in the last four weeks of this campaign to focus on Barack Obama's [voting] record and make sure the voters of Illinois have a chance to make an informed choice.[37]

Confronting Keyes

Keyes made the mistake of airing controversial opinions about political and lifestyle issues, including religion, which is a subject that is usually excluded from politics. A devout Catholic, Keyes immediately attracted attention by focusing on divisive issues such as abortion and homosexuality. Keyes called abortion a "genocide" of blacks in the United States. He compared the act of abortion to terrorism, saying, "What distinguishes the terrorist from the ordinary warrior is that the terrorist will consciously target innocent human life. What is done in the course of an abortion? . . . Someone consciously targets innocent human life."[38]

Keyes also used religion to attack his opponent. He was quoted in the *Chicago Tribune* as saying that "Christ would not vote for Barack Obama because Barack Obama has voted to behave in a

Recruited to replace the disgraced Jack Ryan in the Illinois senate race, controversial Republican candidate Alan Keyes (pictured) would lose the election to Obama.

way that is inconceivable for Christ to have behaved,"[39] referring to votes Obama cast in the state senate against antiabortion legislation.

According to staff reporters John Chase and Liam Ford in the *Chicago Tribune*, Keyes even went so far as to declare that "any Roman Catholic who votes for Democrat Barack Obama would be committing a mortal sin. . . . There [is] no difference between Catholics who support Obama and Germans who voted for the Nazi Party."[40] Yet while Keyes kept making shocking statements about his opponent within Illinois, Obama was about to be catapulted from obscurity into the national spotlight.

"The Audacity of Hope"

By the summer of 2004 John Kerry, a senator from Massachusetts, had taken the lead in the Democratic race and was about to face President George W. Bush in the general election. At the time, the Democratic Party had received criticism for not reaching out to African Americans. After meeting Obama, hearing him speak at a fund-raiser in Chicago, and participating in a town hall meeting with him, Kerry was reportedly impressed with Obama's "passion, eloquence, and charisma," according to one of his aides. After Kerry's advisers predicted that Obama could someday be part of a national ticket, Kerry responded, "He should be one of the faces of our party now, not years from now."[41] The Kerry campaign then asked Obama to give the keynote address at the Democratic National Convention in July in Boston.

Obama recognized Kerry's invitation as an honor and a responsibility and wrote a speech that caught the attention of most of the nation. Titled "The Audacity of Hope," the speech was arguably one of the most memorable moments from the convention. In it, Obama spoke about how the nation's strength could come only from unity, not division:

> Now even as we speak, there are those who are preparing to divide us, the spin masters and negative ad peddlers who embrace the politics of anything goes. Well, I say to them tonight, there is not a liberal America and conservative America—there is the United States of America. There is not a Black America and White America and Latino

Dreams from My Father

After he became president of the *Harvard Law Review*, Obama wrote a memoir titled *Dreams from My Father: A Story of Race and Inheritance*, published in 1995. But it was not until his electrifying speech at the Democratic National Convention in 2004 that interest in Obama's life story and sales of the newly released paperback edition skyrocketed. In the book Obama describes his life growing up and evaluates his place in the world as the son of a Kenyan father.

Obama lost his mother to cancer soon after the 1995 edition was published. In the preface to the 2004 release he writes, "I think sometimes that had I known she would not survive her illness, I might have written a different book—less a meditation on the absent parent, more a celebration of the one who was the single constant in my life. . . . I know that she was the kindest, most generous spirit I have ever known, and that what is best in me I owe to her."

Barack Obama, *Dreams from My Father: A Story of Race and Inheritance.* New York: Three Rivers, 2004.

America and Asian America—there's the United States of America. The pundits like to slice-and-dice our country into Red States and Blue States; Red States for Republicans, Blue States for Democrats. But I've got news for them, too. We worship an awesome God in the Blue States, and we don't like federal agents poking around in our libraries in the Red States. We coach Little League in the Blue States, and yes, we've got some gay friends in the Red States. There are patriots who opposed the war in Iraq, and there are patriots who supported the war in Iraq. We are one people, all of us pledging allegiance to the Stars and Stripes, all of us defending the United States of America. In the end, that's what this election is about. Do we participate in a politics of cynicism, or do we participate in a politics of hope?[42]

Following his memorable keynote address at the 2004 Democratic National Convention, Obama and his wife, Michelle, acknowledge a thunderous ovation.

Political experts and many notable politicians weighed in favorably on Obama's performance. He exited the convention and handily won his own election against Keyes, receiving a whopping 70 percent of the vote while Keyes mustered only 27 percent. According to an analyst writing in the *Economist*, "Republicans may try to blame the result on Alan Keyes, their candidate who was hopeless; they may talk about the meltdown of the state's Republican Party; but they lost the race for the open Senate seat in Illinois for a much simpler reason. In Barack Obama, they were up against a star."[43] Obama's victory put an end to a long and bizarre Senate campaign that left many victims in its wake.

On January 4, 2005, Obama was sworn in as a senator and a member of the 109th Congress as family and friends looked on from the visitors' gallery. Many people considered Obama's victory to be pure luck because of the misfortunes of his running mates. Although some of Obama's hardworking staff objected to this view, Obama himself said, "There was no point in denying my almost spooky good fortune."[44]

Chapter 4

Obama and the Issues

After achieving a landslide victory to become the junior senator of Illinois, Obama became an influential voice on Capitol Hill. As a rising star of the Democratic Party, he was often asked to comment on the policies and actions of President George W. Bush's Republican administration. Yet while he was at times an outspoken opponent of the president's decisions, Obama also proved that his knack for working with members of the opposition party in the state of Illinois was no fluke. His ability to communicate and compromise made a difference in the national debate on the most critical international and domestic issues of the day.

Against the War in Iraq

No issue at the time was as large as the war in Iraq, and Obama always vehemently opposed it. The Bush administration began the war in March 2003 in the belief that Iraq possessed weapons of mass destruction capable of threatening world peace and that the country's leader, Saddam Hussein, an oppressive dictator who ruled his people through intimidation and violence, was also harboring terrorists.

Before the United States invaded Iraq, there was uncertainty about the U.S. military's ability to effectively defeat Hussein's troops without many American casualties, particularly in the capital city of Baghdad, where a bloody standoff was predicted. However,

Iraqi troops were overcome in a matter of weeks with relative ease, and Hussein's regime toppled. Images of an enormous statue of Hussein being yanked to the street by a jubilant mob of Iraqi citizens marked the high point of the invasion. Although Hussein himself fled the capital, he was eventually captured and put on trial as a war criminal.

Yet while the Bush administration was successful in defeating Hussein, no weapons of mass destruction were ever found. Furthermore, there was no evidence linking Hussein and the terrorist

In a 2006 photo in Washington, D.C., Capitol Hill police surround protestors demonstrating against the war in Iraq, a conflict Obama opposed from the beginning.

group al Qaeda, which is led by Osama bin Laden, the mastermind behind the September 11, 2001, terrorist attacks on the World Trade Center and the Pentagon.

Worse, the war continued after Hussein's capture, but it was not waged on a traditional battlefield with identifiable enemy lines; instead, it was fought in a terror zone where numerous insurgent groups detonated bombs and shot at U.S. troops daily. In fact, fewer than one hundred American soldiers were killed before Hussein was taken into custody. But as of early 2009, more than forty-two hundred had been killed according to media reports, and the episodes of violence as Iraq scrambled to form its

Speaking before the Chicago Council on Foreign Affairs in 2005, Obama calls for troop reductions in Iraq.

own democratic government dragged on with no end in sight. What was once an apparent victory had turned into a complex mess of warring tribes, with security far from certain. In a speech to the Chicago Council on Foreign Relations on November 22, 2005, Obama stated, "It has been two years and seven months since the fall of Baghdad and any honest assessment would conclude that the Administration's strategy has not worked."[45]

He went on to say,

> I think . . . that the [Bush] Administration launched the Iraq war without giving either Congress or the American people the full story. . . . I strongly opposed this war before it began, though many disagreed with me at that time. Today, as Americans grow increasingly impatient with our presence in Iraq, voices I respect are calling for a rapid withdrawal of our troops, regardless of events on the ground. But I believe that, having waged a war that has unleashed daily carnage and uncertainty in Iraq, we have to manage our exit in a responsible way—with the hope of leaving a stable foundation for the future, but at the very least taking care not to plunge the country into an even deeper and, perhaps, irreparable crisis. I say this not only because we owe it to the Iraqi people, but because the Administration's actions in Iraq have created a self-fulfilling prophecy—a volatile hotbed of terrorism that has already begun to spill over into countries like Jordan, and that could embroil the region, and this country, in even greater international conflict.[46]

Obama's predictions about the spread of violence and conflict in the region as a result of the continued chaos in Iraq seemed to be coming true in the summer of 2006. With neighboring Iran disregarding calls from the United States and the United Nations to dismantle its nuclear program and war waging between Israel and Lebanon, it appeared that relations between countries in the Middle East and the United States could be strained even further. Obama took a role in international diplomacy as a member of the Senate Foreign Relations Committee, which meant that he would be a key player in negotiations between the United States and countries that threatened world peace.

The Lugar-Obama Act

One important issue that affects the security of the planet is the potential proliferation of weapons of mass destruction. To maintain world peace, countries must work to remove the threat—specifically, the materials used to produce the weapons. According to Obama, the country that warrants the most attention is Russia, the former Soviet Union. He and others believe that the country's stockpiles of enriched uranium, the key element used to create nuclear weapons, could fall into the hands of terrorists. In a speech to the Council on Foreign Relations in November 2005, Obama expressed his concerns:

> Right now, rogue states and despotic regimes are looking to begin or accelerate their own nuclear programs. . . . Some weapons experts believe that terrorists are likely to find enough fissile material to build a bomb in the next ten years—and we can imagine with horror what the world will be like if they succeed. Today, experts tell us that we're in a race against time to prevent the scenario from unfolding. And that is why the nuclear, chemical, and biological weapons within the borders of the former Soviet Union represent the greatest threat to the security of the United States— a threat we need to think seriously and intelligently about in the months to come.[47]

To accomplish these goals, Obama worked closely with Senator Richard Lugar, a Republican from Indiana who coauthored the Nunn-Lugar Act of 1991, which in turn led to the Cooperative Threat Reduction Program. Since its formulation, the program brought about the deactivation and destruction of 6,828 nuclear warheads, 865 nuclear air-to-surface missiles, 29 nuclear submarines, and 194 nuclear test tunnels as well as thousands of intercontinental ballistic missiles. Obama acted as Lugar's Democratic counterpart on amendments and expansions to the program.

Obama and Lugar traveled to Russia in 2005 and spent time in Ukraine and Azerbaijan, two states on the fringe of the former Soviet Union, where nuclear, chemical, and biological weapons were created and stored. Obama observed that because of antiquated

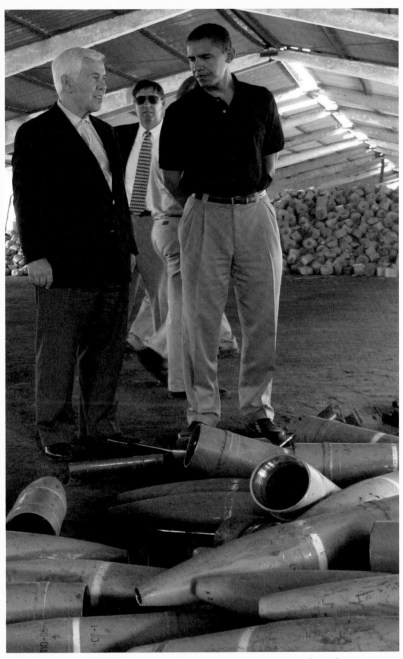

During their 2005 trip to Russia, Senators Richard Lugar and Barack Obama visit a Ukrainian warehouse containing defused shells and land mines.

technology, old yet dangerous conventional weapons in Ukraine will take sixty years to be properly dismantled. In the meantime, it is entirely possible that such weapons could be distributed to violent pockets in Asia and Africa, where terrorists or rogue governments would welcome the chance to unleash them.

In an effort to prevent such makeshift weapons manufacturing, Obama worked with Lugar to draft S.2566, the Lugar-Obama Act. Introduced on April 6, 2006, its purpose was to expand the State Department's ability to detect and stop weapons and the development and trafficking of materials to create weapons of mass destruction. Specifically, the act would help secure lightweight antiaircraft missiles. The State Department estimates that as many as 750,000 of these shoulder-fired air defense systems are in arsenals worldwide and that more than forty civilian aircraft have been hit by such weapons since the 1970s.

The potential threat of materials in the hands of terrorists is just one of the major international issues on which Obama focused. Another was the seemingly separate yet actually intertwined subject of energy and oil production, perhaps the most vital matter affecting American peace and economic prosperity.

The Price of Power

Russia and the Middle East are often the focal points of U.S. foreign policy because these regions produce the vast majority of the world's oil, the lifeblood of the nation's economy. Oil fuels nearly all of the transportation in the United States, yet very little of this oil is produced domestically. This has created a dependence on foreign oil, which has led to troublesome compromises with Arab nations that are not ideologically aligned with the United States. And those nations that are supposedly American allies in the Middle East are subjected to terrorist activities targeting oil supplies.

Obama's approach to solving the U.S. dependence on foreign oil is two pronged: reduce consumption and fund initiatives to rapidly develop alternative fuel sources. He is a proponent for the advancement of biofuels, such as ethanol, as well as other technologies that harness fuel from agricultural products, including corn stalks and switch grass. He says, "With technology we have

In 2005 Obama introduced the Healthcare for Hybrids Act, to encourage America's "Big Three" automakers to manufacture hybrid vehicles such as this Ford Escape.

on the shelves right now and fuels we can grow right here in America, by 2025 we can reduce our oil imports by over 7.5 million barrels per day—an amount greater than all the oil we are expected to import from the entire Middle East."[48]

In addition to developing incentives to make more fuel-efficient cars, which would have a positive impact on the environment, Obama tried to enact legislation that would provide government funding for technologies to produce alternative fuels that could reverse the effects of global warming.

Hot About Global Warming

Many scientists believe that Earth's climate is changing in dangerous ways, a future problem that President Obama is tackling now. The changes result from the excessive consumption of fossil fuels, used in practically every building, factory, home, and motor vehicle on the planet. The emissions from these fuels create a "greenhouse effect" that allows heat from the sun to reach

Earth but then traps infrared radiation escaping from Earth's surface. In theory, this will lead to higher-than-average temperatures that will cause huge portions of ice to melt in places, such as the North Pole, South Pole, and Greenland. As the ice melts and breaks loose into the oceans, water levels around the world will rise so that coastlines are gradually submerged by an ever-growing sea. Additional problems may include abnormally warm temperatures that alter plant and animal life within various ecosystems and more frequent and more powerful tropical storms and tornadoes, which derive their strength from warm, wet climates.

While in the U.S. Senate, Obama was critical of the Bush administration's claim that there was no scientific proof of global warming. He pointed to countries that accepted global warming as scientific fact and changed their lifestyles to reverse the effect. He reminded people of Japan's efforts in slowing oil consumption by making and buying millions of fuel-efficient cars and Brazil's commitment to investment in biofuels, approaches he advocated for the United States, which would increase the volume of renewable fuels required to be blended into a gasoline. Such fuels are derived from sources such as plants or come from the conversion of solar energy into chemical energy.

Obama offered ways in which the government can make investing in alternative energy more attractive, such as forming an energy technology program within the Defense Department that could provide loan guarantees and funding for plans that develop and market biofuels commercially. Such a plan would decrease the risk inherent in investing in speculative technologies and yet-to-be-established markets. He also advocated several other actions, including setting a renewable fuel standard and creating an alternative diesel standard, with the goal of blending 65 billion gallons of alternative fuels per year with the current petroleum supply by 2025. He also said that the federal government should purchase only flexible-fuel vehicles, and he supports legislation that would ensure that within ten years every new car sold in the United States is a flexible-fuel vehicle. To support that initiative, he recommended giving automakers a one-hundred-dollar tax credit to install flexible-fuel tanks in their cars, an amount which equals the cost of the upgrade.

Obama pushed for legislation that would reduce harmful emissions from factories and provide incentives for companies to switch over to cleaner energy alternatives such as solar power. He has also made strides toward supporting the improvement of cleaner ways to burn coal, which is the most abundant source of energy in the United States.

Expanding Coal Use

In June 2006 Barack Obama and Senator Jim Bunning introduced the Coal-to-Liquid Fuel Promotion Act of 2006. The legislation, which was never passed, would have created tax incentives for coal-to-liquids (CTL) technology and the construction of CTL plants, making CTL an environmentally friendly energy resource in the United States.

Coal is an abundant domestic resource. When gasified in the CTL process, it is refined into diesel. This final product is cleaner than regular diesel because of the removal of sulfur and nitrogen. According to Obama:

> The people I meet in town hall meetings back home would rather fill their cars with fuel made from coal reserves in Southern Illinois than with fuel made from crude reserves in Saudi Arabia. We already have the technology to do this in a way that's both clean and efficient. What we've been lacking is the political will. This common sense, bipartisan legislation will greatly increase investment in coal-to-liquid fuel technology, which will create jobs and lessen our dependence on foreign oil. Illinois Basin Coal has more untapped energy potential than the oil reserves of Saudi Arabia and Kuwait combined. Instead of enriching the Saudis, we can use these reserves to bring a renaissance for Illinois coal.

Quoted in Sourcewatch.org, "Statement by Obama on introducing S.3325, the "Coal-To-Liquid Fuel Promotion Act of 2006," with Senator Jim Bunning (R-KY), in June 2006." http://www.sourcewatch.org/index.php?title=Barack_Obama_statements_on_coal

Smart on Education

In addition to energy and environmental issues, education is another of Obama's particular interests. A product of two excellent universities, he recognizes that many students may not be as fortunate as he was. With tuition costs rising at alarming rates, young Americans from middle- to lower-income families may not be able to afford college. Parents and students can take out loans,

Tennis star Venus Williams reads about good dental hygiene habits to students in Head Start, a program that Obama strongly supports.

but that means more debt for families to pay off along with other weighty financial obligations, such as a mortgage and health-care.

Obama recognizes these financial hardships and has taken steps to make education more accessible to everyone. In April 2005 he introduced the Higher Education Opportunity Through Pell Grant Expansion (HOPE) Act. Its purpose is to amend the Higher Education Act of 1965 and make college more affordable by increasing the maximum amount of Pell Grant awards from $4,050 to $5,100 a year, nearly 26 percent.

It is estimated that more than 5 million undergraduate students depend on Pell Grants to help them defray college costs, and 85 percent of Pell Grant recipients come from households with an income below forty thousand dollars. Obama described the current problems with Pell Grants at a press conference at the Southern Illinois University at Edwardsville: "Pell grants, the government's primary financial aid for college students, only cover 23 percent of the total cost of an average four year public institution . . . and they have not been indexed to the rising price of tuition or inflation. As a result, the current limit is worth $700 less than it was worth 30 years ago."[49]

Political Optimist

It is not only education at the college level that concerns Obama. He is also committed to ensuring full funding of government-sponsored programs such as Head Start, which provide education, medical, dental, and parent-involvement programs to impoverished children and their families. Because of his commitments to early childhood education and to accessible, high-quality day care, Obama was the 2005 recipient of the Harold Blake Walker Award, which is given to individuals for their contributions to human services or social reform.

The next year, in March 2006, Obama introduced S.2441, a bill to authorize resources for the development of twenty so-called innovation districts. These districts would emphasize teacher recruitment, training, and retention, including pay increases to high-performing teachers and financial incentives to teachers willing to work in low-income schools. In a speech titled "Twenty-First

Hard Knocks at Knox

During a June 2005 commencement speech at Knox College in Illinois, Obama shared with graduates the importance of a good education in today's economy. He said:

> While most of us have been paying attention to how much easier technology has made our own lives—sending e-mails back and forth on our Blackberries, surfing the Web on our cell phone . . . a quiet revolution has been breaking down barriers and connecting the world's economies. . . . Now business not only has the ability to move jobs wherever there's a factory, but wherever there's an Internet connection. Countries like India and China realized this. . . . They can compete with us on a global scale. The one resource they needed were skilled, educated workers. So they started schooling their kids earlier, longer, with a greater emphasis on math and science and technology, until their most talented students realized they don't have to come to America to have a decent life—they can stay right where they are. The result? China is graduating four times the number of engineers that the United States is graduating. . . . If you've got the skills, you've got the education, and you have the opportunity to upgrade and improve both, you'll be able to compete and win anywhere. If not, the fall will be further and harder than it ever was before.

Barack Obama, Commencement Address at Knox College, Galesburg, IL, June 4, 2005. http://www.americanrhetoric.com/speeches/barackobamaknoxcollege.htm.

Century Schools for a Twenty-First Century Economy," Obama points out, "Teaching is one of the only professions where no matter how well you perform at your job, you're almost never rewarded for success."[50] In an innovation district, teachers would be given mentors for more support and more time with their students in the form of longer days or summer school. Those schools that fail to meet pre-defined expectations would be eliminated from the program.

Whether the issue is education, energy, the environment, or foreign relations, in his first term as a U.S. senator, Obama focused his attention and efforts on key domestic and international issues that held tremendous significance for the future of the United States. Clearly, he was a leader with his vision trained on the horizon. Because of his forward-looking, optimistic approach to politics, many people looking ahead to the 2008 presidential election had their eyes on Obama.

Chapter 5

The Campaign for President

Barack Obama was a little-known state legislator until July 27, 2004, when he delivered the keynote address at the Democratic National Convention. Millions of people who watched him on television were mesmerized by his eloquence and the drama of his life story. His stirring speech and election four months later as the fifth African American senator in U.S. history instantly transformed him into a political star.

Political groups around the country were anxious to meet Obama, who was making a name for himself as a charismatic and intelligent leader. In his first term as a U.S. senator, Obama quickly demonstrated his political savvy, his interest in making changes in Washington, and his willingness to work hard for issues important to him and to the people who elected him to office. When a reporter asked him about his rapid rise to political prominence, Obama responded, "I think what people are most hungry for in politics right now is authenticity."[51]

By late 2006 many people were urging him to run for president. Obama was intrigued by the idea but realized the campaign posed many risks to himself and his family. Obama was not sure whether he could win, and a failed campaign would doom any future chance to be elected president. He also knew he would be the target of personal attacks that could hurt his family.

Because his campaign would drastically affect his family, Obama asked his wife, Michelle, whether he should run. They discussed it in December 2006 while vacationing in Hawaii with daughters

Malia and Sasha. Obama said that despite concerns about the campaign, Michelle told him to run:

> Her initial instinct was to say no. [We] just talked it through. It wasn't as if it was a slam dunk for me. I think part of the reason she agreed to do it was because she knew that she had veto power, that she and the girls ultimately mattered more than my own ambitions in this process, and if she said no we would be OK.[52]

When Obama decided to enter the race, he instantly became one of the front-runners to win his party's presidential nomination.

A Presidential Contender

When the sun rose on February 10, 2007, the temperature in Springfield, Illinois, was only seven degrees above zero. The freezing weather did not stop fifteen thousand people from gathering outside a historic building in the Illinois capital to hear Barack Obama deliver the most important speech of his life. Wearing a heavy dress coat but not gloves or a hat despite the bitter cold, his breath materializing in chilly white puffs as he spoke, Obama announced he was running for president:

> [In] the shadow of the Old State Capitol, where [Abraham] Lincoln once called on a divided house to stand together, where common hopes and common dreams still live, I stand before you today to announce my candidacy for president of the United States.[53]

The Old State Capitol is a historically accurate reconstruction of the statehouse that housed the Illinois government from 1839 to 1876. On June 16, 1858, Abraham Lincoln accepted the Republican Party nomination for the U.S. Senate in that building. In one of his most famous speeches, Lincoln warned that the United States had to end slavery, because some states supported slavery while others opposed it, and it was dividing the nation. "A house divided against itself cannot stand," Lincoln said. "I believe this government cannot endure, permanently half slave and half free."[54] Two years later when Lincoln was elected president,

Upon his February 10, 2007, announcement that he would run for president of the United States, Obama became an instant front-runner in the race. Here, he greets thousands of supporters at a campaign stop only one day after his announcement.

he kept the nation united during the Civil War, which was fought mainly over the issue of slavery, and a Union victory, followed by the Thirteenth Amendment, finally abolished that cruel practice.

On February 10, 2007, Illinois was witnessing history again as an African American, who would probably have been a slave in 1858, announced that he wanted to be president. Obama said he sought the Democratic presidential nomination because he was the only candidate who would dramatically change the domestic and foreign polices of President George W. Bush that were hurting the nation:

> I recognize that there is a certain presumptuousness in this, a certain audacity to this announcement. I know that I have not spent a long time learning the ways of Washington, but I have been there long enough to know that the ways of Washington have to change.[55]

The theme of "change" became the heart of Obama's campaign. Rapid and dramatic change was something Obama had experienced personally since bursting onto the national political scene at the 2004 Democratic National Convention in Boston, Massachusetts.

Victory and Then Defeat

The 2008 Democratic campaign was historic because it featured the first black and the first female candidates who could be elected president. Joining Obama in making history was New York senator Hillary Clinton, whose husband, Bill, had been president from 1993 to 2001. The Reverend Herman Bing was one of many people troubled that both firsts came in the same campaign. Bing, the African American pastor of Carpentersville Baptist Church in North Augusta, South Carolina, admitted "I really hate that they had to run at the same time in the same election. It just makes [it] very stressful for folk like me."[56]

Obama and Clinton were among more than a half-dozen Democrats, including Delaware senator Joe Biden and John Edwards, the party's 2004 vice presidential candidate, who were seeking the nomination. In the first poll of candidates in November 2006,

Clinton ranked first with 28 percent of likely voters and Obama second with 17 percent. Despite Obama's solid showing, many political analysts did not believe he could win. They claimed his inexperience—he had been a senator for only two years—and racism, which would deny him some whites' votes, would weaken him too much to defeat Clinton. Even worse, as the first black candidate considered to have a chance to win, some supporters were warning him that racists might try to assassinate him. There were death threats against him, and the U.S. Secret Service started protecting Obama in May 2007, eight months before the first primary.

But Obama quickly showed his political strength by raising $24.8 million in the first quarter of 2007—more money than anyone except Clinton—and drawing huge, enthusiastic crowds to political rallies. On February 12, several thousand supporters at Iowa State University in Ames, Iowa, heard Obama say he needed their help to win: "I can't do this alone. I'm going to need all of you, and I hope that you guys decide [working for Obama] is something that's worth doing."[57]

In the fall of 2007 Obama still trailed Clinton in national polls by 20 to 30 percent. What those polls did not reflect was the strong campaign organization he had in Iowa, where so many people had answered his call for help. Volunteers were important because Iowa, which on January 3, 2008, hosted the nation's first primary contest, was a caucus primary. In a caucus primary, voters have to register and attend small gatherings of fellow Democrats, many of which were held in private homes. To be successful in a caucus, candidates need an army of volunteers to contact possible voters and get them to caucus sites. Obama's campaign had thousands of supporters, many of them young people involved in politics for the first time. They distributed campaign literature and made telephone calls supporting Obama. On election night, they helped people attend caucuses by giving free rides and babysitting.

The hard work of volunteers and the excitement Obama generated among voters paid off with a stunning victory. Obama won the primary with 38 percent of the vote while Edwards placed second with 30 percent and Clinton ran a disappointing and somewhat surprising third with 29 percent. That night Obama told cheering supporters: "[At] this defining moment in history, you have done what

Clinton cited Obama's lack of experience and claimed that, even though she had only been a senator a few years longer than Obama, she was much more prepared to be president. Clinton claimed her role as former First Lady gave her more White House and foreign policy experience. She called Obama's speeches, which were generating enthusiasm among voters "just words."[59] Bill Clinton used his popularity with African American voters to try to persuade them that his wife would be a better advocate for blacks than Obama. The Clinton campaign tried to argue that Obama was elitist and out of touch with the majority of the black population.

Obama forcefully challenged Clinton in televised debates but mostly refrained from running negative political ads about her. Obama concentrated on telling voters what he would do to change U.S. policy, like ending the Iraq War, making health care more affordable, and lessening political bickering between the Republican and Democratic parties. Obama was also still introducing himself to voters and explaining his unique heritage. He talked to voters about his unusual name and the fact that he was racially mixed. Obama would jokingly tell his audience,

> When I first ran for [the Illinois] state Senate [people] would call me 'Yo Mama.' And I'd have to explain, 'No, it's O-bama—that my father was from Kenya, from Africa, which is where I got the name . . . and that my mother was from Kansas, which is why I talk the way I do.[60]

Despite his background, there were few negative incidents in the early primaries over his race or his father's nationality. Eventually, however, both became campaign issues.

Problems for Obama

In February 2008 a picture taken of Obama in traditional Somali clothing appeared first on the Internet and then in the news media. Obama had dressed in the clothes, which look similar to clothes worn by Muslims in the Middle East, while visiting Africa two years earlier. The photo fed rumors circulating in the conservative media and among some voters that Obama was a Muslim and sympathetic to Muslim terrorists. This story seems to have started because Obama's middle name is Hussein—a common Muslim name. Some suggested that the Clinton campaign released the photo in order to feed the negative stereotypes circulating about Obama and to improve Clinton's chances, but this was never proved. Obama ignored the picture, and it never became a serious campaign issue.

Another problem arose in March over negative statements the Reverend Jeremiah Wright had made about whites. Wright is the African American pastor of Trinity United Church of Christ in Chicago. Obama, who attended that church, was criticized for his relationship with Wright, whom Obama called his spiritual mentor.

When Wright's comments ignited a media firestorm, Obama knew he had to do something to calm the furor over Wright's remarks. On March 18, Obama discussed Wright in a major speech about race in Philadelphia. Obama condemned Wright's remarks but noted that many whites have negative attitudes about blacks. Although Obama admitted racial tension still exists between blacks and whites, he said he believed the situation will improve:

> I have asserted a firm conviction—a conviction rooted in my faith in God and my faith in the American people—that working together we can move beyond some of our old racial wounds, and that in fact we have no choice if we are to continue on the path of a more perfect union.[61]

Obama's speech was hailed for the intelligent way it summed up the racial divide between the two races. It reminded historians of a speech John F. Kennedy had given in 1960 when he was running for president. Kennedy was Roman Catholic. He had to defend his religion from Protestant critics who claimed the pope, the leader of the Catholic Church, would influence the policy decisions he made. Kennedy, an eloquent speaker with whom Obama is often compared, was so persuasive in explaining his religious beliefs that his Catholicism ceased to be a political problem.

In a similar manner, Obama's speech quieted racial concerns about his candidacy. But even though he began collecting a string of primary victories, Obama remained locked in a bitter struggle with Clinton for the nomination.

"Yes. We. Can."

Even after Clinton resurrected her campaign by winning the New Hampshire primary, Obama never lost faith he would win. In his concession speech on January 8 in Nashua, New Hampshire, Obama congratulated Clinton. Then Obama told cheering supporters he could still win:

> We will remember that there is something happening in America; that we are not as divided as our politics suggests; that we are one people; we are one nation; and together, we will begin the next great chapter in America's story with three words that will ring from coast to coast; from sea to shining sea — Yes. We. Can.[62]

Obama repeated the phrase *yes we can* over and over to explain what he would do if elected and how he would win the nomination and the presidency. "Yes we can" became a mantra for his campaign, which was growing stronger across the nation thanks to thousands of people who were volunteering to work for him and donating money. Obama's powerful campaign organization and growing appeal to voters led to an important victory in South Carolina's primary election on January 26, when he garnered 55 percent of the vote to 27 percent for Clinton. Three days later Senator Ted Kennedy, a highly respected and influential figure in the Democratic Party, endorsed Obama over Clinton. It was a serious blow to Clinton's campaign.

On February 5, dubbed Super Tuesday, twenty-three states and territories voted. Obama captured thirteen primaries on Super Tuesday and then won the next eleven primaries to consolidate his dominance over Clinton, who was having so much trouble keeping up with Obama's fund-raising that she and her husband personally loaned her campaign $5 million. On February 12, Obama won big victories in Maryland, Virginia, and the District of Columbia to fly past Clinton in the delegate count 1,210 to 1,188. The nomination went to the candidate with the most delegates, which candidates got by winning primaries or the endorsement of superdelegates, elected officials and party members elected to that position. It marked the first time Obama had more

Democratic presidential candidate Barack Obama accepted his party's nomination at the Democratic National Convention in Denver, Colorado, on August 28, 2008.

delegates than Clinton; he would never again trail in the delegate count.

Clinton kept battling for the nomination even though it would have been difficult to overtake Obama's delegate lead. Some Democrats wanted her to quit running. They argued that her candidacy was forcing Obama to spend money he could use in the general election against the Republican nominee. Fellow Democrats also feared that Clinton's continuing political attacks would weaken Obama with voters. Clinton did not quit until June 7, four days after Obama had wrapped up enough delegates (2,118) in the final primaries to capture the nomination.

Obama accepted the nomination on August 28 in Denver with a dramatic speech to eighty-four thousand people jammed into a football stadium. Obama said he was ready to meet the greatest challenge facing the nation. The greatest challenge, however, was no longer the Iraq War, the overriding issue when the campaign began. Instead it was the weakening U.S. economy, which Obama said was harming millions of people:

> Tonight, more Americans are out of work and more are working harder for less. More of you have lost your homes and even more are watching your home values plummet. More of you have cars you can't afford to drive, credit card bills you can't afford to pay, and tuition that's beyond your reach.[63]

Obama claimed he was better suited than Arizona senator John McCain, the Republican presidential candidate, to deal with the economy. The general election would be decided by whether voters believed that statement.

Obama Versus McCain

Like Obama, McCain defied predictions by political experts and won his party's nomination. Unlike Obama, McCain won so many primaries early that he had secured the Republican nomination by March over rivals Mike Huckabee, Mitt Romney, and Rudy Giuliani.

McCain posed a stark contrast to Obama. A Vietnam War hero hailed for his bravery as a prisoner after his plane was shot down,

McCain wanted to keep American troops in Iraq. He had also supported President Bush's policies for eight years. Obama based his campaign on bringing American troops home from Iraq and overturning many Bush policies. There was also a disparity in the ages of the candidates. McCain was seventy-two years old, and many voters wondered whether he could handle the stress of being president. If elected, McCain would be the oldest person to ever become president. McCain also seemed old-fashioned to some voters when he admitted that he does not use a computer. Obama loves technology and used it to help raise money for his campaign by having a strong presence on social networking sites on the Web. He even kept in touch with supporters via text messages.

Rising discontent over the Iraq War and Bush's growing unpopularity gave Obama an early lead over McCain. A June 10 Gallup poll showed 46 percent of voters supporting Obama to 43 percent for McCain. Obama was drawing such huge crowds at home and even overseas—two hundred thousand people heard him speak on July 24 in Berlin, Germany—that Republicans became worried about his popularity. To mock his growing fame, they ran a television advertisement suggesting that Obama was just a pop celebrity like Britney Spears and Paris Hilton but not someone suited to lead the nation. Obama dismissed the ad as an example of negative Republican campaigning:

> One of their general strategies is to try to turn strengths into weakness. The enthusiasm and involvement [of people in] my campaign, I consider a strength. People have not come out because of my speechmaking. They've come out because they understand what's at stake in this election.[64]

And Obama was soon able to claim McCain did not understand the election's most important issue—the failing U.S. economy. At a rally in Jacksonville, Florida, on September 15, McCain admitted to about three hundred people that "the American economy is in crisis [but then claimed] the fundamentals of our economy are strong."[65] The comment was perhaps the biggest mistake McCain made in his campaign.

Presidential candidates John McCain and Barack Obama went head-to-head at several debates in September and October 2008.

McCain Missteps

McCain had been commenting on the latest development in the continuing deterioration of the economy—the collapse of Lehman Brothers, one of the nation's largest investment banks, and the sale of Merrill Lynch, another investment firm. Hours later at a rally in Pueblo, Colorado, Obama told three thousand people that McCain's comment showed that he did not understand why the economic downturn happened. Claimed Obama:

> I don't think John McCain gets what's happening [to the economy]. Why else would he say, today of all days—he said this just this morning—that the fundamentals of the economy are still strong? Senator McCain, what economy are you talking about?[66]

The worst recession in eight decades was caused by a variety of factors, including the cost of gasoline (it soared to more than four dollars a gallon), home mortgage defaults that weakened banks, a huge decline in the value of stocks, and massive layoffs by financially troubled businesses. Those economic problems had become the top concern of voters. McCain's comment made it seem like he did not realize how much the weakened economy was hurting people who were losing jobs, homes, and investment savings that they needed to live on. The result was that more voters began to believe Obama was better suited than McCain to salvage the economy.

McCain also weakened his campaign, many feel, by choosing Alaska governor Sarah Palin as his vice presidential running mate. The importance of experience was an issue the McCain camp often used against Obama. Sarah Palin, it turned out, had no national political experience. Governor of Alaska was the highest post she had achieved, and she had not held the office very long. People questioned whether she had the knowledge or experience to be vice president. More importantly, they questioned what would happen if the elderly McCain died or was unable to continue as president because of health problems and Palin became president. Palin reinforced these concerns by appearing uninformed and flustered in her first television interviews after being chosen to run with McCain.

Victory Through Technology

One of the biggest advantages Barack Obama had over his two main opponents—Hillary Clinton and John McCain—was his campaign's superior use of technology. The Obama campaign effectively harnessed the Internet with www.barackobama.com, the most powerful political campaign site ever. Once someone registered on the site, his campaign kept e-mailing updates and requests for donations. That effort helped Obama raise a record $750 million, more than twice as much as McCain. The site also helped link his supporters in various states and around the country so they could get together and work for him. Social networking sites also helped Obama's campaign attract thousands of volunteers. Obama focused on communicating with MySpace and Facebook users and started a YouTube channel people could subscribe to and find out about his campaign. Obama is a dedicated BlackBerry user and his campaign used cell phones in new ways. When Obama picked Delaware senator Joe Biden as his vice presidential running mate, his campaign announced it first in text messages sent to supporters who had submitted their telephone numbers. The campaign kept sending them other news about the campaign and made appeals for donations. His campaign also effectively used its main Web site and other sites to counter political attacks, often just a few hours after the attacks were made.

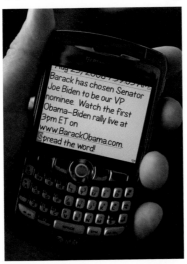

Obama embraced the use of technology during his presidential campaign.

When the general election began after the conventions, the race between Obama and McCain was expected to be close. But by early fall, Obama was ahead in the polls, and his advantage continued to grow as voters decided he was best-suited to lead the nation. His growing advantage over McCain allowed Obama on October 23 and October 24 to visit his 86-year-old grandmother, Madelyn Dunham, who was dying of cancer. Because the trip to Hawaii took so long, he had to suspend his campaign both days. In Honolulu, Obama praised the woman who had helped raise

After a strong victory at the polls on November 4, 2008, President-elect Barack Obama gives his acceptance speech to a massive crowd at Chicago's Grant Park.

him: "She has really been the rock of the family, the foundation of the family. Whatever strength and discipline that I have, it comes from her."[67]

Obama was saddened when he had to return to the campaign because he knew he would probably never again see the woman he lovingly called "Toot," a shortened version of Tutu, the Hawaiian word for grandmother. She died on November 2, two days before her grandson won a landslide election to become the nation's first black president.

On November 4 Obama tallied 69,456,897 votes (52.92 percent of those cast) and won 365 electoral votes to 59,934,814 (45.67 percent) and 173 electoral votes for McCain. Political pundits credited Obama's win to several possible factors. The weakening economy was one. The United States seemed unified in a

widespread desire for change after the Republican policies of the Bush administration. This put the Republican McCain at a disadvantage. McCain's choice of Sarah Palin as a running mate turned off some voters as a poor choice and a somewhat irresponsible decision. Many said that voters trusted Obama to turn the economy around and to restore hope.

"Dream of Our Founders"

The night he was elected, Obama addressed thousands of jubilant people at Grant Park in Chicago just a few miles from his Hyde Park home. He told them, "If there is anyone out there who still doubts that America is a place where all things are possible; who still wonders if the dream of our founders is alive in our time; who still questions the power of our democracy, tonight is your answer."[68]

His meaning was clear. By electing a black president, voters had shown the world that the Declaration of Independence's promise of equality for all people had finally come true.

Chapter 6

President Obama

In addition to being the first African American president, Barack Obama is also the third president—the others were Calvin Coolidge and Chester A. Arthur—to take the oath of office twice. On January 20, 2009, Supreme Court Justice John G. Roberts Jr. misplaced the word *faithfully* when he administered the oath to Obama. Although constitutional experts agree that Obama did not need to take the oath again to legalize his presidency, Obama had Roberts administer it again the next night in the White House. When Roberts correctly finished the second swearing in he said, "Congratulations, again," and Obama replied, "Thank you, sir."[69]

Obama was finally president. In the two months between the election and the inauguration, Obama had prepared for his new position, and he hit the ground running.

A Quick Start

On November 7, 2008, Obama held his first news conference as president-elect. Although Obama's landslide victory over Republican senator John McCain three days earlier had repudiated the policies of President George W. Bush, Obama told reporters that Bush was still in charge of the nation. "The United States," Obama said, "has only one government and one president at a time, and until January 20th of next year, that government is the current administration."[70]

Obama, however, had already begun preparing for the day he would assume the presidency by choosing people to head key government agencies. His most surprising pick was Senator Hillary Clinton as secretary of state. He chose Clinton even though she had waged a tough, bitter campaign against him. Obama said she was the person best suited to help him deal with foreign policy issues.

Obama began meeting with his advisers to find ways to help the nation's economy recover from its worst economic downturn since the Great Depression. In the fall of 2008, the Bush administration had created a $750-billion plan to help banks and investment firms

Among President Obama's first presidential acts was signing an executive order on January 22, 2009, closing the U.S. military prison at Guantánamo Bay, Cuba.

deal with the downturn. Obama and his economic team now crafted an $800-billion plan to help citizens struggling with financial problems, especially the more than 2 million people who had lost jobs. The new plan included income tax breaks, more money for unemployment benefits, and massive spending on domestic programs to create jobs. Obama began building public support for the plan by discussing its importance in news conferences and public appearances before he became president. During a January 16, 2009, visit to a manufacturing plant in Bedford Heights, Ohio, Obama warned that swift action was needed to fix the economy:

> It's not too late to change course—but only if we take dramatic action as soon as possible. The first job of my administration is to put people back to work and get our economy moving again.[71]

Obama submitted his proposal to Congress before he took office, and just eight days after he became president the House passed the measure on January 28. The Senate passed the bill on February 10. The Senate and House then argued over the scope of the final legislation before finally agreeing on a $787-billion bill to help revive the nation's weakened economy. Obama signed the measure into law on February 17 in Denver, Colorado. It was the largest single expenditure of money in U.S. history. Obama predicted the bill would begin helping Americans suffering from the financial downturn, but had this reminder for Americans:

> Now, I don't want to pretend that today marks the end of our economic problems. Nor does it constitute all of what we're going to have to do to turn our economy around. But today does mark the beginning of the end: the beginning of what we need to do to create jobs for Americans scrambling in the wake of layoffs, the beginning of what we need to do to provide relief for families worried they won't be able to pay next month's bills, the beginning of the first steps to set our economy on a firmer foundation, paving the way to long-term growth and prosperity.[72]

Obama was also planning new programs to help the ailing auto industry and homeowners who were having trouble paying their mortgages. But the swift action on the economic stimulus bill had historians comparing Obama to President Franklin D. Roosevelt, who in 1932 initiated a flurry of bills in his first hundred days in office to help the nation recover from the Great Depression. Roosevelt biographer H.W. Brands saw a similarity between Obama and Roosevelt. He said, "To the extent there is a parallel, the lesson would be: Take advantage of this opportunity because the nation is looking to you [for help]."[73]

The new president took many other actions in his first few weeks in office, most of them aimed at changing Bush policies. Obama said he would close the military prison at the U.S. Naval Station Guantánamo Bay, Cuba, which had become controversial for holding Iraqi war prisoners without allowing them a chance to prove their innocence, and reaffirmed his stand against torturing military prisoners. Obama also began working to heal relations with Muslim countries, which had deteriorated because of the Iraq War. In his first interview as president, Obama told Al Arabiya, an Arab television network, he will open talks with Muslim nations and others that oppose the United States, a diplomatic tactic Bush had shunned. The fact that Obama gave Al Arabiya the honor of broadcasting his first interview was considered a sign of his sincerity in wanting to improve relations with Muslim countries.

Domestically, Obama announced he would introduce legislation to encourage American automakers to build cars that get better gasoline mileage to curb U.S. dependency on foreign oil and improve air quality. On January 29, Obama signed his first bill, a new law making it easier for workers to sue for pay discrimination. On the same day, the Senate, at Obama's urging, approved a measure to expand health coverage to more children. Obama also began working on other measures to help Americans suffering financially, from lowering mortgage costs to providing low-interest loans for small businesses.

A national Gallup poll on January 25 showed 68 percent of Americans approved of Obama's actions. Only John F. Kennedy's early approval rating of 72 percent in 1961 is higher. Obama, however, was gearing up to make even more changes. After his inauguration, Obama told his senior staff members and advisers

Obama and the Economy

Political analysts believe a major reason Barack Obama was elected president was that more people believed he could revive the shattered U.S. economy than John McCain. In October 2008, Joe Klein wrote in *Time* magazine that Obama did that by being more effective than McCain in explaining the economic problem and how it should be solved:

> The difference between them was made clear in the second question of the [October 15, 2008], debate—a fellow named Oliver Clark wanted to know how the Wall Street bailout would help his friends who were in trouble. McCain's answer was all over the place and obscure in a classic Washington way; he detoured into blaming [financial institutions] and pointing his finger at Obama and his cronies: for supporting [them]. Obama, by contrast, brought the bailout home in simple language: "Well, Oliver, first, let me tell you what's in the rescue package for you. Right now, the [financial] credit markets are frozen up, and what that means, as a practical matter, is that small businesses and some large businesses just can't get loans. If they can't get a loan, that means that they can't make payroll. If they can't make payroll, then they may end up having to shut their doors and lay people off." I don't think McCain has answered a single question with that sort of clarity in these debates.

Joe Klein, "The Obama Surge," *Time*, October 20, 2008, p. 301.

that he was excited to be in a position to make life better for Americans. Said Obama: "What an opportunity we have to change this country. The American people are really counting on us now. Let's make sure we take advantage of it."[74]

New foreign and domestic policies were not the only changes Obama was expected to create. Many people believed his election would also lead to improved race relations.

A New Racial Attitude

Obama's victory stunned many historians and average citizens who had believed racism was still too strong in the United States for a black person to be elected president. Some considered Obama's election proof that the nation had become less racist. Many people also believed Obama's presidency would further improve the nation's racial climate. In a magazine article published

Support for America's first African American president crossed racial boundaries. Pictured here is a crowd gathered in New York City to watch a large-screen viewing of the inauguration of Barack Obama.

in October 2007, Obama himself had speculated on the effect his election could have:

> As president, obviously the day I am inaugurated, the racial dynamics in this country will change to some degree. If you've got Michelle as first lady, and [daughters] Malia and Sasha running around on the South Lawn [of the White House], that changes how America looks at itself. It changes how White children think about Black children, and it changes how Black children think about Black children.[75]

On the day of Obama's inauguration, Tyreese Holmes claimed Obama's victory had already had a positive impact on his sons, twelve-year-old Malik Williams and ten-year-old Jalen Williams. Holmes, an African American, had taken them to Centennial Olympic Park in Atlanta, Georgia, to watch the historic event on a giant screen television. Holmes told a reporter that Obama's election had already raised his expectations for what his sons could accomplish. Said Holmes: "The sky's the limit for them now. Malik talks about being an astronaut, and seeing [Obama] become president, [now] I can encourage him to be an astronaut. It feels like anything is possible."[76]

Introduction: The First African American President

1. Barack Obama, "The Challenges We Face Are Real," *Milwaukee Journal Sentinel*, January 21, 2009.
2. Quoted in Diane Ravitch, *The American Reader: Words That Moved a Nation*. New York: HarperCollins, 1991, p. 20.
3. Obama, "The Challenges We Face Are Real."
4. Quoted in Ravitch, *The American Reader*, p. 334.
5. Quoted in Dahleen Glanton, "Living King's Dream on the National Mall," *Chicago Tribune*, January 21, 2009.
6. Quoted in Traci Watson, "Slave History Adds Poignancy to Oath Site," *USA Today*, January 20, 2009.

Chapter 1: A Fateful Beginning

7. Barack Obama, *Dreams from My Father: A Story of Race and Inheritance*. New York: Three Rivers, 2004, p. 15.
8. Obama, *Dreams from My Father*, p. 17.
9. Obama, *Dreams from My Father*, p. 126.
10. Obama, *Dreams from My Father*, p. 51.
11. Obama, *Dreams from My Father*, p. 52.
12. Obama, *Dreams from My Father*, pp. 69–70.
13. Quoted in *O, The Oprah Magazine*, "Oprah's Cut with Barack Obama," November 2004, www.oprah.com/omagazine/20 0411/omag_200411_ocut.jhtml.
14. Obama, *Dreams from My Father*, pp. 79–80.
15. Obama, *Dreams from My Father*, p. 99.
16. Obama, *Dreams from My Father*, pp. 100–101.
17. Noam Scheiber, "Race Against History," *New Republic*, May 31, 2004, p. 22.

Chapter 2: The Streets of Chicago

18. Obama, *Dreams from My Father*, p. 115.
19. Obama, *Dreams from My Father*, p. 134.
20. Obama, *Dreams from My Father*, p. 136.

21. Obama, *Dreams from My Father*, p. 139.
22. Obama, *Dreams from My Father*, pp. 164–65.
23. Obama, *Dreams from My Father*, p. 242.
24. Obama, *Dreams from My Father*, p. 276.
25. Scott Turow, "The New Face of the Democratic Party—and America," *Salon*, March 30, 2004, http://dir.salon.com/story/news/feature/2004/03/30/obama/index.html.
26. Quoted in Amanda Ripley, David E. Thigpen, and Jeannie McCabe, "Obama's Ascent," *Time*, November 15, 2004, p. 74.
27. William Finnegan, "The Candidate," *New Yorker*, May 31, 2004.
28. Finnegan, "The Candidate."
29. Quoted in Scheiber, "Race Against History," p. 22.
30. Turow, "The New Face of the Democratic Party—and America."
31. Quoted in Anne Marie Tavella, "Taping Murder Interrogations Wins Early Senate Support," *Chicago Daily Herald*, March 5, 2003.
32. David Mendell, "Obama's Record a Plus, a Minus," *Chicago Tribune*, October 8, 2004.
33. Finnegan, "The Candidate."

Chapter 3: Senator Obama

34. Quoted in Finnegan, "The Candidate."
35. Finnegan, "The Candidate."
36. Alan Keyes, interviewed by Robert Novak, *Crossfire*, CNN, December 15, 1999.
37. Quoted in Mendell, "Obama's Record a Plus, a Minus."
38. Quoted in Natasha Korecki, "Keyes Likens Abortion to Terrorism." *Chicago Sun-Times*, August 17, 2004.
39. Quoted in Liam Ford and David Mendell, "Jesus Wouldn't Vote for Obama, Keyes Says," *Chicago Tribune*, September 8, 2004.
40. Quoted in John Chase and Liam Ford, "Keyes Presses Catholic Voters," *Chicago Tribune*, November 1, 2004.
41. Quoted in Jill Zuckman and David Mendell, "Obama to Give Keynote Address," *Chicago Tribune*, July 15, 2004.
42. Barack Obama, keynote address, Democratic National Convention, Boston, MA, July 27, 2004.

43. *Economist*, "Obama's Second Coming: Victory for a Rising Star," November 6, 2004, p. 33.

44. Barack Obama, *The Audacity of Hope: Thoughts on Reclaiming the American Dream*. New York: Crown, 2006 , p. 9.

Chapter 4: Obama and the Issues

45. Barack Obama, "Moving Forward in Iraq," speech to the Chicago Council on Foreign Relations, Chicago, IL, November 22, 2005.

46. Obama, "Moving Forward in Iraq."

47. Barack Obama, "Nonproliferation and Russia: The Challenges Ahead," speech to the Council on Foreign Relations, Washington, DC, November 1, 2005.

48. Barack Obama, "Energy Security Is National Security," speech, Governor's Ethanol Coalition, Washington, DC, February 28, 2006.

49. Quoted in Brandee J. Tecson, "Obama's HOPE Act: A Bid to Make College More Affordable," MTV News, April 1, 2005, www.mtv.com/news/articles/1499404/20050401/index.jhtml? headlines=true.

50. Barack Obama, "Twenty-first Century Schools for a Twenty-first Century Economy," speech, Chicago, IL, March 13, 2006. http://www.obamaspeeches.com/057-21st-Century-Schools-for-a-21st-Century-Economy-Obama-Speech.htm.

Chapter 5: The Campaign for President

51. Quoted in Amanda Ripley, "Obama's Ascent," *Time*, November 15, 2005, p. 76.

52. Quoted in Evan Thomas, "How He Did It," *Newsweek*, January 21, 2008, p. 40.

53. Barack Obama, speech announcing presidential candidacy, Springfield, IL, February 10, 2007. www.barackobama.com/2007/02/10/remarks_of_senator_barack_obam_11.php.

54. Abraham Lincoln, "House Divided," speech, Springfield, IL, June 16, 1858. http://www.historyplace.com/lincoln/divided.htm.

55. Obama, speech announcing presidential candidacy.

56. Quoted in Jon Meacham, "Letting Hillary Be Hillary," *Newsweek*, November 17, 2008, p. 31.

57. Quoted in Judy Keen, "Obama Comes Out Swinging in Iowa," *USA Today*, February 12, 2007.

58. Quoted in Susan Page and Jill Lawrence, "Obama, Huckabee Reshape the Race with Wins in Iowa; Setbacks for Clinton and Romney, Hope for Edwards as N.H. Looms," *USA Today*, January 4, 2008.

59. Quoted in David Von Drehle, "The Five Faces of Barack Obama," *Time*, September 1, 2008, p. 32.

60. Quoted in Noam Scheiber, "Race Against History," p. 22.

61. Barack Obama, "A More Perfect Union," speech, Constitution Center, Philadelphia, PA, March 18, 2008. www.huffingtonpost.com/2008/03/18/obama-race-speech-read-th_n_92077.html.

62. Barack Obama, speech on New Hampshire primary, Nashua, NH, January 8, 2008. www.barackobama.com/2008/01/08/remarks_of_senator_barack_obam_82.php.

63. Barack Obama, speech accepting Democratic nomination for president, Democratic Convention, Denver, CO, August 28, 2008. www.barackobama.com/2008/08/28/remarks_of_senator_barack_obam_108.php.

64. Quoted in Von Drehle, "The Five Faces of Barack Obama," p. 36.

65. Quoted in Carol E. Lee, "McCain Says Fundamentals of Economy Strong Despite Threat," *Gainesville (FL) Sun*, September 16, 2008.

66. Quoted in Dean Toda, "3,000 at Obama Rally in Pueblo; Economic News Provides Fodder for Candidate Speech," *Colorado Springs Gazette*, September 16, 2008.

67. Robert Barnes, "Obama Visits Grandma Who 'Was His Rock,'" *Washington Post*, October 25, 2008, page A-2.

68. Barack Obama, speech on election night, Grant Park, Chicago, IL, November 4, 2008. http://obamaspeeches.com/E11-Barack-Obama-Election-Night-Victory-Speech-Grant-Park-Illinois-November-4-2008.html.

Chapter 6: President Obama

69. Quoted in Donald G. Savage, "The President Does It Over, Without a Hitch This Time, to Remove Any Doubt About the Legitimacy of His Term," *Los Angeles Times*, January 22, 2009.

70. Barack Obama, press conference, Chicago, IL, November 7, 2008. http://blogs.suntimes.com/sweet/2008/11/president elect_obama_first_pre.html.

71. Quoted in *Milwaukee Journal Sentinel*, "Obama Wants Green Economy," January 17, 2009.

72. Quoted in Sheryl Gay Stolberg and Adam Nagourney, "Recovery Measure Becomes Law and Partisan Fight Endures," *New York Times*, February 18, 2009, p. A17.

73. Quoted in Craig Gilbert, "Finding Focus Amid Frenzy," *Milwaukee Journal Sentinel*, February 1, 2009.

74. Quoted in Liz Sidoti, "Obama Breaks from Bush, Avoids Divisive Stands," *Corpus Christi (TX) Caller-Times*, January 24, 2009. http://news.yahoo.com/s/ap/20090124/ap_on_go_pr_wh/obama_first_week.

75. Quoted in Gwen Ifill, "The Candidate," *Essence*, October 2007, p. 226.

76. Quoted in Judy Keen, "Feelings Reach Heightened Pitch in USA," *USA Today*, January 21, 2009.

Important Dates

1961

Barack Hussein Obama Jr. is born in Honolulu, Hawaii, on August 4.

1979–1981

Obama attends Occidental College in Los Angeles, California.

1983

Obama graduates from Columbia University in New York, New York.

1983–1987

Obama works as a community organizer in Chicago, Illinois.

1990

Obama becomes the first African American president of the *Harvard Law Review*.

1991

Obama graduates magna cum laude from Harvard Law School.

1992

Obama directs a voter registration drive in Chicago. Marries Michelle Robinson.

1995

Obama's memoir, *Dreams from My Father: A Story of Race and Inheritance*, is published.

1996

Obama is elected to the Illinois state senate.

1997–2004

Obama represents the Thirteenth District of Chicago as an Illinois senator.

2000

Obama runs unsuccessfully in the Democratic primary for Illinois' first congressional district against incumbent representative Bobby Rush.

2004

Obama gives the keynote address at the 2004 Democratic National Convention in Boston, Massachusetts, on July 27. Obama's memoir is rereleased in paperback.

2005

Obama is sworn in as a U.S. senator for Illinois on January 4. In April he proposes his first Senate bill, the Higher Education Opportunity Through Pell Grant Expansion Act of 2005 (HOPE Act).

2007

Obama launches his presidential campaign in Springfield, Illinois, on February 10.

2008

Obama wins the Iowa caucus on January 3.

Obama accepts the Democratic nomination for president on August 28.

Obama is elected president of the United States on November 4.

2009

Obama is sworn in as the forty-fourth president of the United States on January 20.

For More Information

Books

Marlene Targ Brill, *Barack Obama: Working to Make a Difference.* Minneapolis: Millbrook, 2006. A biography of Obama that discusses his parents, childhood, education, and political and public life.

James Daley, *Great Speeches by African Americans: Frederick Douglass, Sojourner Truth, Dr. Martin Luther King, Jr., Barack Obama, and Others.* Mineola, NY: Dover, 2006. An anthology of speeches by influential people in the African American community, including Barack Obama's 2005 Knox College commencement address.

Barack Obama, *The Audacity of Hope: Thoughts on Reclaiming the American Dream.* New York: Crown, 2006. In this book, Obama recounts his early experiences as a senator and explains his vision of more authentic politics.

Barack Obama, *Dreams from My Father: A Story of Race and Inheritance.* New York: Three Rivers, 1995. In this memoir, Obama discusses his life growing up with his mother and grandparents in Hawaii and his struggles to connect with his African heritage and identity despite the absence of his Kenyan father.

Web Sites

Biography.com (www.biography.com). This Web site offers biographies and photos of well-known people, including celebrities, actors, sports figures, politicians, and historical figures. The site offers an up-to-date biography of Barack Obama with several videos, including his keynote address at the 2004 Democratic National Convention and a brief excerpt from his presidential acceptance speech on November 4, 2008.

Facebook (www.facebook.com/barackobama). Barack Obama's Facebook page includes a brief biography, photos, videos, and links to articles. A Facebook account is required for access to detailed information.

On the Issues: Every Political Leader on Every Issue (www.on theissues.org). This Web site provides information about America's leaders and their positions on various issues. It also offers information about the 2008 presidential campaign, including the presidential debates.

Organizing for America (www.barackobama.com). Organizing for America is a project of the Democratic National Committee. Its Web site offers articles, a blog, videos, Barack Obama merchandise, and information on Obama's Economic Recovery Plan.

The White House (www.whitehouse.gov). This Web site provides information about Barack Obama and the people and policies of his administration. The site also offers details about the White House and its history, information on every administration since George Washington, and a comprehensive section about the U.S. government.

Through Pell Grant Expansion (HOPE) Act (2005), 63
Holmes, Tyreese, 90
Hull, Marson Blair, Jr., 41–42
Hussein, Saddam, 52, 53
Hynes, Dan, 42

I
Iraq War, 52–55

J
Jackson, Andrew, 8
Jefferson, Thomas, 7, 8

K
Kennedy, John F., 74
Kennedy, Ted, 75
Kenya, 31–32
Kerry, John, 48
Keyes, Alan, 46–48, 47
King, Martin Luther, Jr., 9
Klein, Joe, 88

L
Lincoln, Abraham, 67, 69
Loving v. Virginia (1967), 14
Lugar, Richard, 57
Lugar-Obama Act (2006), 58

M
Matthews, Kgosie, 39
McCain, John, 77–80, *78*, 88
Mikva, Abner, 32

O
Obama, Barack Hussein, Jr., *13, 54*
on addressing global warming, 60–61
on Altgeld Gardens, 28–29
approval ratings of, 87
birth of, 15

on coal-to-liquids technology, 61
as community organizer, 24–26
in debate with John McCain, 79
on decision to enroll in law school, 31
on the economy, 88
educational policies of, 62–65
on ending U.S. dependence on imported oil, 58–59
with family, *7, 34, 41, 71*
gives keynote address at Democratic National Convention, 48–49
giving acceptance speech, *82*
at Harvard, *33*
on his family and decision to run for president, 67
on his grandmother, 83
on his mother, 49
on his struggle with identity, 21
as Illinois state senator, 34–35, 37–38
on importance of education, 64
at Inaugural, *7*
inaugural speech of, 6
on Iraq War, 55
launches political career, 34–35
loses congressional bid to Rush, 35–37
meets his father, 19–20
at Occidental College, 22–23
on passage of his economic stimulus bill, 86
in presidential campaign, *68*
at Punahou Academy, 18–19
on racism and voting, 72
with Richard Lugar, *57*

About the Authors

Mark and Sherri Devaney are married writing partners who seek inspirational topics to write about and found one in Barack Obama, their second book for Lucent Books. Mark, a former teacher and journalist, is a business development professional for an engineering firm. Sherri is an editor who focuses on educational and medical publishing. They live in Sparta, New Jersey, with their biggest inspirations, Sean and Jeremy.

Michael V. Uschan has written seventy books, including Lucent Books' *Life of an American Soldier in Iraq*, for which he won the 2005 Council for Wisconsin Writers Juvenile Nonfiction Award. Uschan began his career as a writer and editor with United Press International, a wire service that provides stories to newspapers, radio, and television. Uschan considers writing history books a natural extension of the skills he developed in his many years as a journalist. He and his wife, Barbara, reside in the Milwaukee suburb of Franklin, Wisconsin.